Contents

JUDAISM

Chapter 1
Judaism: Beliefs and teachings 4

Chapter 2
Judaism: Practices 23

Chapter 3
Exam practice: Judaism 44

THEMES

Chapter 4
Theme A: Religion, relationships and ethical studies 62

Chapter 5
Theme B: Religion, peace and conflict 81

Chapter 6
Theme C: Religion, human rights and social justice 101

Chapter 7
Exam practice: Themes 123

How to use this book

Start by writing your name on the front cover – this workbook has been designed for you!

You can use it as you progress through your GCSE Religious Studies course, or as part of your revision for the final exam. It's full of different activities to help you learn by doing, not just reading.

This workbook covers Judaism for Paper 2Y, Section A and religious, philosophical and ethical studies for Paper 2A, Section B, which is Component 2: Perspectives on faith.

This refers to pages in this student book. You can go back to your student book to read about the topic in more depth.

Activity 1.1: The Trinity [SB] pages 2–3

Working your way through these activities will help strengthen your understanding of some of the key topics in your GCSE course.

Follow the instructions and write your answers in the space provided.

_____
_____
_____
_____
_____

There are lots of blank lines for you to write in your answers.

Key terms [SB] pages 2–3

It's important to get to grips with some of the specialist language that we use when talking about religion. You will need to recognise these 'key terms' because they may turn up in an exam question. And you will also need to know how to use them in your answers. These activities will help you to feel confident using religious language. Test yourself regularly on these terms.

Key Terms Glossaries appear at the end of chapters 1, 2, 4, 5 and 6.

Key Terms Glossary
You can collect the meanings of key terms here so you can refer to them at any time. You will also be creating a useful revision tool.

Sources of religious belief and teaching pages 2–3

The 5-mark question in the exam asks you to 'refer to scripture or another source of Christian/Jewish belief and teaching.' These activities will help you to memorise short quotations from religious sources, such as the Bible or Tenakh and also explain what these quotations mean.

This will also be helpful for the 4-mark and 12-mark questions because you can refer to religious teachings to add detail to the points you make, and to back up your arguments.

> **TIP**
>
> Keep an eye out for these TIPS. They contain useful advice, especially to help with your exam.

Exam practice

If you see an arrow running down the side of a box, that means the activity or activities you are doing will end with an exam practice question. These are like the questions that you will encounter in your exams. Use the information and guidance from the activities to practise the 1, 2, 4, 5 and 12-mark questions.

Finally, there are two whole chapters dedicated to

Exam practice

There are five different types of question in the AQA exam paper – the **1**, **2**, **4**, **5** and **12-mark** questions.

Work your way through these chapters to find out what each question will look like and how it is marked.

There are some activities that will help you to understand what the examiner is looking for in an answer, and activities that practise the skills you should be demonstrating. You should then be ready to have a go at a few questions yourself.

> **WHAT WILL THE QUESTION LOOK LIKE?**
>
> This explains the command words that the question will use.

> **HOW IS IT MARKED?**
>
> This explains what the examiner will be looking for in your answer.

> **REMEMBER...**
>
> This provides useful tips to help raise your marks.

All answers can be found online at www.oxfordsecondary.co.uk/aqa-rs-answers, so you can mark what you've done.

Once you have filled out this workbook, you will have made your own book to revise from. That's why your name is on the cover.

Chapter 1: Judaism: Beliefs and teachings

Activity 1.1: The nature of God: God as One

pages 212–213

Fill in the gaps in the sentences below using the words provided. (There are more words than gaps – you will have to decide which ones to leave out.)

Tenakh   Adonai   polytheistic   Latin   love   creator   monotheistic
diversity   one   Hebrew   God   Shema   Talmud   patience

Judaism is a _____ religion, which means a belief in only one God who is the source of all Jewish morality, beliefs and values. Jews believe that the scriptures in the _____ explain God's role in Jewish history. However, there is considerable _____ within Judaism regarding how the Tenakh should be interpreted and how the faith is practised.

Some Jews show respect by not writing the word _____. Instead they use G-d as a sign of respect. God's name written in _____ cannot be erased or destroyed, or said out loud. Instead the word _____ is used, which means 'my Lord'.

The _____ is an important Jewish prayer taken from Jewish scriptures. It expresses the belief that there is only _____ God, and that Jews should show _____ and loyalty towards God.

Sources of religious belief and teaching

page 213

A Learn the following quotation about the Jewish belief of one God.

> "Hear, O Israel! The LORD is our God, the LORD is one. You shall love the LORD your God with all your heart and with all your soul and with all your might."
>
> *Deuteronomy 6:4–5*

This quotation is the opening of the Shema. It emphasises that God is one, and that humans should show loyalty to him in every part of their lives.

Fill in the gaps below. It will help you to learn the quotation if you say the whole thing out loud every time you write it.

"Hear, O _____! The LORD is our _____, the LORD is one. You shall _____ the _____ your God with all your _____ and with all your _____ and with all your _____."

4

Chapter 1: **Judaism: Beliefs and teachings**

Now cover up the text on the opposite page and have a go at writing out the whole quotation from memory.

"_____

_____

_____

_____ "

B Answer the questions below about the quotation you have just learned.

1. Which part of the quotation reminds Jews that they believe in only one God? Write this out below.
_____
_____

2. What does the second part of the quotation tell Jews about how they should live their lives?
_____
_____
_____

Activity 1.2: Jewish and Christian beliefs about the nature of God

 pages 212–215

In the table below there are some Jewish beliefs about the nature of God and God's role in creation. Do Christians believe the same? In the right-hand column, explain how Christian beliefs are either similar or different.

TIP
In your exam you might be asked to compare Jewish and Christian beliefs about monotheism and God as creator.

Jewish belief	Christian belief
Jews believe that there is only one God, who is a single being that cannot be divided.	
Jews believe that they should only worship one God, by showing complete love and loyalty towards him.	
Jews believe that God created the universe from nothing.	
In the Torah, Genesis tells how God took six days to create the universe. Many Orthodox and ultra-Orthodox Jews believe this actually happened, while other Jews believe that life in the universe evolved over a much longer period of time.	

5

Chapter 1: Judaism: Beliefs and teachings

Activity 1.3: The nature of God: God as creator

pages 214–215

A Mark the following statements about the nature of God as true or false.

	True	False
Genesis tells how God created the universe and rested on the seventh day; Jews remember this day of rest on Wednesdays.	☐	☐
Jews believe that God is omnipotent, which means all knowing.	☐	☐
Jews believe that God is omnipresent, which means being everywhere at all times.	☐	☐
Jews believe that evil was created by the devil.	☐	☐
Jews believe that God gave humans free will to be able to choose between right and wrong.	☐	☐
Jews believe that God sustains the universe today.	☐	☐

B Now write out a correct version of the statements that you have marked as false.

_____
_____
_____
_____
_____
_____
_____
_____

Exam practice

Now answer the exam question below.

Which **one** of the following means that God is omniscient? **[1 mark]**

Put a tick (✓) in the box next to the correct answer.

A God is present everywhere ☐

B God continues to sustain and keep his creation going ☐

C God is all knowing ☐

D God is all powerful ☐

Chapter 1: **Judaism: Beliefs and teachings**

Activity 1.4: The nature of God: God as lawgiver and judge

pages 216–217

Tick the correct answer for each of the questions below.

1. At which festival do Jews believe that God's judgement happens?
   - ☐ Shabbat
   - ☐ Pesach
   - ☐ Rosh Hashanah
   - ☐ Bar Mitzvah

2. What is the name for the 613 laws found in the Torah?
   - ☐ Mitzvot
   - ☐ Talmud
   - ☐ Ten Commandments
   - ☐ Tenakh

3. What does Shekhinah mean?
   - ☐ God is merciful as well as a fair judge.
   - ☐ There is only one God.
   - ☐ People are created to have free will.
   - ☐ God's divine presence.

4. What is the Tabernacle?
   - ☐ The scrolls kept in the synagogue.
   - ☐ Where the Shabbat candles are kept in a Jewish home.
   - ☐ A prayer used daily by Jews.
   - ☐ A portable structure that housed the divine presence of God.

Activity 1.5: The nature of God

pages 212–217

Answer the following questions about the nature of God.

1. Which of the following ways to describe God do you think might be most important to Jews today? Circle your choice.

   Creator   One   Judge   Lawgiver

2. Now write down **two** reasons for your choice.

   1 _____
   _____

   2 _____
   _____

TIP
There is no correct answer as such here, but as you decide, think about the reasons for your choice. For example, can you think of any sources of Jewish belief and teaching that support your choice? Do you think one of these descriptions might have more of an impact on how Jews practise their faith today?

3. Can you think of any arguments against your choice, such as a reason why Jews might think the other descriptions are more important? Write down one or two of these arguments here.

   _____
   _____
   _____
   _____

7

Chapter 1: Judaism: Beliefs and teachings

Exam practice

Use your answers to the previous two activities to help you answer this exam question.

'God as creator is the most important belief about God for Jews.'
Evaluate this statement. In your answer you should:

- give reasoned arguments to support this statement
- give reasoned arguments to support a different point of view
- refer to Jewish teaching
- reach a justified conclusion.

> **TIP**
> It is acceptable to only partly agree or disagree with a statement if you can explain why. A vague statement such as 'there are strengths and weaknesses for both' would not be a real conclusion. Give your reasons clearly for why you feel some arguments are strong and some are weak.

[12 marks]
[+3 SPaG marks]

! REMEMBER...

Focus your answer on the statement you are asked to evaluate.

- Try to write at least three paragraphs – one with arguments to support the statement, one with arguments to support a different point of view, and a final paragraph with a justified conclusion stating which side you think is more convincing, and why.
- Look at the bullet points in the question, and make sure you include everything that they ask for.
- The key skill that you need to demonstrate is evaluation. This means expressing judgements on the arguments that support or oppose the statement, based on evidence. You might decide an argument is strong because it is based on a source of religious belief and teaching, such as a teaching from the Tenakh, or because it is based on scientific evidence. You might decide an argument is weak because it is based on a personal opinion, or a popular idea with no formal evidence. You can use phrases in your chains of reasoning such as 'I think this a convincing argument because…' or 'In my opinion, this is a weak argument because…'.

Chapter 1: **Judaism: Beliefs and teachings**

Activity 1.6: Jewish beliefs about life after death

pages 218–219

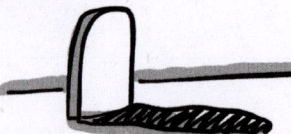

A The table below gives four Jewish beliefs about the afterlife. In the right-hand column of the table, say whether all Jews agree with these beliefs or not. If there is an alternative belief, explain what it is.

Belief	Do all Jews agree? If not, what is the alternative belief?
Gan Eden (heaven) is where Jews will be with God.	
Gan Eden is a physical place.	
Jews are judged by God as soon as they die.	
Jews will be resurrected after they die.	

B Now answer the question below.

Give **two** reasons why Jewish beliefs about the afterlife vary.

1 _____
_____

2 _____
_____

Sources of religious belief and teaching

page 218

A Learn the following quotation.

> **Blessed are You, L**ORD **our God, King of the universe, the True Judge.**

Jews make this blessing to God when they hear that a loved one has died.

Fill in the gaps below. It will help you to learn the quotation if you say the whole thing out loud every time you write it.

"_____ are You, _____ our God, King of the

_____, the True _____."

10

Chapter 1: **Judaism: Beliefs and teachings**

"_____
_____"

B Now answer the following question.

1. What do you think this blessing shows about Jewish beliefs about the afterlife?

_____
_____
_____
_____

Activity 1.7: The nature and role of the Messiah

 pages 220–221

The statements below are muddled up. Copy them into the correct box below to show whether they are believed by most Orthodox Jews or most Reform Jews.

- The Messiah will bring world peace.
- There will not be a Messiah.
- A future Messianic age will be achieved by people working together.
- The Messiah will gather all Jews back to Israel.
- Everyone should work together for peace rather than waiting for the Messiah.
- In every generation there is a descendant of King David who has the potential to be the Messiah.

TIP
For your exam it is also useful to know how Jewish and Christian beliefs about the Messiah differ. The main difference is that Christians believe Jesus was the Messiah, but Jews do not.

Most Orthodox Jews' views about the Messiah	Most Reform Jews' views about the Messiah
• _____ _____ _____	• _____ _____ _____
• _____ _____ _____	• _____ _____ _____
• _____ _____ _____	• _____ _____ _____

Now cover up the text on the opposite page and have a go at writing out the whole quotation from memory.

Chapter 1: **Judaism: Beliefs and teachings**

Exam practice

Now answer this exam question.

Explain **two** Jewish beliefs about the nature and role of the Messiah. [4 marks]

_____
_____
_____
_____
_____
_____
_____
_____
_____

Activity 1.8: Abraham's journey

pages 222–223

Fill in the gaps in the sentences below using the words provided. (There are more words than gaps – you will have to decide which ones to leave out.)

| Promised | binding | descendants | Moses | Ur | monotheist | idols |
| circumcised | nations | covenant | Egypt | Israel | Exalted | Isaac |

Abraham came to believe there was only one God – he became a _____ who rejected worshipping

_____.

God told Abraham to leave his home in _____ and travel with his family to Canaan. When he arrived,

God told him to look around and said, 'for I give all the land that you see to you and your offspring forever' (*Genesis* 13:15). This

promise means that Canaan (present-day _____) is known as the _____ Land.

God made a _____ with Abraham that he would be the father of many _____

if he would 'walk in My ways and be blameless' (*Genesis* 17:1). Abraham agreed to this and _____

himself and all the males in his household.

God gave Abraham and his wife Sarah a baby boy, called _____. He can be seen as a gift from God to

mark the covenant between God and Abraham. As a result of this, Abraham had many _____.

12

Chapter 1: **Judaism: Beliefs and teachings**

Exam practice

Use your answers to Activity 1.8 to help you answer the following question.

Give **two** Jewish beliefs about Abraham and his covenant with God. **[2 marks]**

1 _____
_____

2 _____
_____

Activity 1.9: The escape from Egypt

pages 224–225

The following boxes tell the story of how the Jews escaped from Egypt, but they have been muddled up. Number the boxes below from 1 to 9 to show in which order the events happened. The first one has been done for you.

- ( ) God told Moses to ask the Pharaoh to release the Jewish slaves.
- ( ) God sent a number of plagues to Egypt.
- ( ) The Pharaoh refused to let the Jewish slaves go.
- ( ) The last plague was the death of the firstborn child in every Egyptian family.
- ( ) Moses was rescued from the river Nile and brought up in the Egyptian palace.
- ( ) God parted the Sea of Reeds (or Red Sea) to help the Jews to escape.
- ( ) God met Moses and spoke to him through a burning bush.
- (1) The Jews were slaves in Egypt.
- ( ) The Jews travelled to Mount Sinai, where Moses received the Ten Commandments.

13

Chapter 1: **Judaism: Beliefs and teachings**

Activity 1.10: The Ten Commandments

pages 224–225

A Tick the following statements to show which of them come from the Ten Commandments.

One of the Ten Commandments?

Do not worship sculptured images ☐

Honour your father and mother ☐

Attend the synagogue ☐

Pray every day ☐

Do not murder ☐

Do not eat pork ☐

B Now answer the following questions.

1. The Jews promised to follow the Ten Commandments as part of the covenant at Sinai. What did God promise as part of this covenant?

   _____
   _____
   _____
   _____

2. Which of the Ten Commandments do you think a student in your school might find hardest to follow today? Give a reason for your choice.

   _____
   _____
   _____
   _____

3. Cover the text in part A and try to write out **three** of the Ten Commandments from memory.

   _____
   _____
   _____
   _____

Chapter 1: **Judaism: Beliefs and teachings**

Activity 1.11: Key moral principles in Judaism

pages 226–227

A Read this text about justice, healing the world and kindness to others. Five of the sentences are incorrect. As you read, highlight these five sentences (the first one has been done for you, so there are four left to find).

Judaism provides guidance on how to live in a way that pleases God. ==Three important principles are justice, destroying the world and kindness to others.==

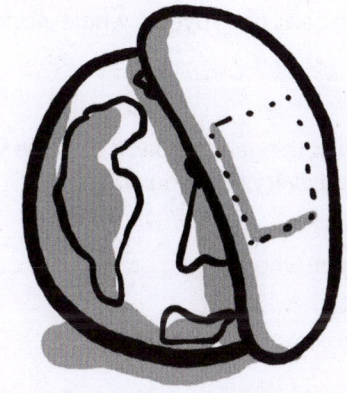

The prophets explained that God loves justice. Micah said that God wants people to 'do justice and love goodness'. This means that Jews should only care about themselves. Also the Torah gives guidance on how to treat the poor and vulnerable to help achieve justice.

Secondly, Jews believe they should be involved in God's work to sustain the world by healing the world. One example of this is volunteering for a social justice or environmental charity. A Jewish charity offering practical support to people in need is Oxfam. Some Jews additionally believe that healing the world involves obeying the mitzvot and becoming closer to God, for example through prayer.

Finally, selfishness is an important concept in Judaism. Many laws in the Torah spell out how Jews should treat others kindly, demonstrating that the Torah positively encourages kind actions. The Torah also forbids negative actions such as giving to charity or helping a friend.

In summary, we can see that these three aspects of Jewish morality work together. Justice is linked to acting in a way that supports the needy; kindness to others is healing the world in one's own community.

B Now rewrite the five sentences below so they are correct. The first one has been done for you.

Sentence 1: *Three important principles are justice, healing the world and kindness to others.*

Sentence 2: _____

Sentence 3: _____

Sentence 4: _____

Sentence 5: _____

Chapter 1: **Judaism: Beliefs and teachings**

Sources of religious belief and teaching

page 228

A Learn the following quotation.

> "He who destroys one life, the Scripture considers him as if he has destroyed a whole world."
>
> *Sanhedrin* 4:5

This quotation shows the importance of saving life in Judaism. It says that killing one person is as bad as destroying a whole world.

Fill in the gaps below. It will help you to learn the quotation if you say the whole thing out loud every time you write it.

"He who destroys one _____, the _____ considers him as if he has _____ a whole _____."

Now cover up the text above and have a go at writing out the whole quotation from memory.

"_____

_____"

B Answer the following question.

1. Why does this quotation encourage Jews to save lives?

_____

_____

_____

Activity 1.12: Pikuach nefesh

pages 228–229

Fill in the gaps in the sentences below about the Jewish obligation to save life. Use the words provided. (There are more words than gaps – you will have to decide which ones to leave out.)

minyan   Talmud   God   nefesh   end   Shabbat   Amidah
    sacred   surgery   preserve   rabbis   body   sea

Jews believe that life is _____ and only _____ can give life or take it away. However, humans have a responsibility to help _____ life. This responsibility is called pikuach _____ and takes precedence over most other Jewish laws.

16

One example of this is related to transplant _____. Many Jews feel that although they believe the _____ should be buried intact, the possibility of giving someone a new life by donating an organ is more important.

Another example is that _____ rules can be set aside if it is in order to save a life. The _____ has several examples of when this is acceptable. These include rescuing a child from the sea and putting out a fire that is endangering life.

Exam practice

Use your answers to the previous two activities to answer this exam question.

Explain **two** Jewish teachings about pikuach nefesh.

Refer to scripture or another source of Jewish belief and teaching in your answer. **[5 marks]**

Chapter 1: **Judaism: Beliefs and teachings**

Activity 1.13: The mitzvot

 pages 230–231

Answer the questions below about the mitzvot in sentences.

1. What is the term that means God gives people the opportunity to make decisions about right and wrong for themselves?

2. What is the literal meaning of the word 'mitzvah'?

3. How many mitzvot are there in the Torah?

4. How many of the Ten Commandments are about a person's relationship with God?

5. Some mitzvot guide how people should treat each other. Give an example of a topic they might cover.

6. Why do Jews believe it is important to follow the mitzvot?

Key terms

 pages 214–231

A These terms and their meanings are muddled up. Write out the meanings in the correct order in the second table opposite.

Torah	Jewish rules or commandments
Mitzvot	The Jewish holy day of the week, starting shortly before sunset on Friday and continuing to nighttime on Saturday
Messiah	The first section of the Tenakh, which forms the Jewish written law
Shekhinah	A commentary on the Torah
Talmud	The 'anointed one'; a leader of the Jews expected to live on earth sometime in the future
Shabbat	The divine presence of God

18

Chapter 1: **Judaism: Beliefs and teachings**

Torah	
Mitzvot	
Messiah	
Shekhinah	
Talmud	
Shabbat	

B Now write the correct term beside each meaning. For an extra challenge, cover up the rest of this activity and try to see if you can recall the words from memory.

A commentary on the Torah	
The first section of the Tenakh, which forms the Jewish written law	
Jewish rules or commandments	
The 'anointed one'; a leader of the Jews expected to live on earth sometime in the future	
The Jewish holy day of the week, starting shortly before sunset on Friday and continuing to nighttime on Saturday	
A commentary on the Torah	

19

Chapter 1: Judaism: Beliefs and teachings

Key Terms Glossary

As you progress through the course, you can collect the meanings of useful terms in the glossary below. You can then use the completed glossaries to revise from.

To do well in the exam you will need to understand these terms and include them in your answers. Tick the shaded circles to record how confident you feel. Use the extra boxes at the end to record any other terms that you have found difficult, along with their definitions.

- ◯ I recognise this term
- ◯ I understand what this term means
- ● I can use this term in a sentence

Covenant

Creator

Free will

Gan Eden

God as One

Healing the world

Judge

Judgement

Justice

Kindness to others

Lawgiver

Chapter 1: Judaism: Beliefs and teachings

Liberal Judaism

Messiah

Mitzvot

Monotheism

Orthodox Judaism

Pikuach nefesh

Promised Land

Reform Judaism

Resurrection

Sanctity of human life

Shekhinah (Divine Presence)

Shema

Chapter 1: **Judaism: Beliefs and teachings**

Sheol

Sinai

Tenakh

Ten Commandments

Torah

Chapter 2: Judaism: Practices

Activity 2.1: The importance of the synagogue

 pages 234–235

Fill in the gaps in the sentences below using the words provided. (There are more words than gaps – you will have to decide which ones to leave out.)

| Orthodox | music | shul | Latin | worship | Hebrew |
| social | community | library | menorah | Reform | minyan |

A synagogue is a place where Jews meet for prayer, _____ and study. Jews can pray anywhere, but some prayers can only be said in the presence of a _____.

In _____ synagogues this is ten men over the age of 13, whereas in _____ Judaism, women can be included as well.

Another name for the synagogue is _____, which means school or place of study.

Some synagogues provide classes for learning _____, which is the language used in the Tenakh and in prayers. Most synagogues have a good _____ that adults can use to improve their understanding of the faith.

The synagogue is the centre of a Jewish _____. As well as a centre for prayer and education, it is a _____ centre with regular activities and events, some of which are for charity.

23

Chapter 2: Judaism: Practices

Activity 2.2: Interior features of a synagogue

 pages 236–237

The statements below are muddled up. They describe different features that can be found inside a synagogue. Copy them out into the correct boxes below.

- A reminder that the altar was the central feature of the Temple courtyard.
- This is also known as the Aron Hakodesh.
- A light that is kept burning at all times.
- A raised platform, usually in the centre of the synagogue.
- Symbolises God's presence and is never put out.
- Usually set into the wall facing Jerusalem.
- Used when reading the Torah.
- Where the sacred Torah scrolls are kept.
- A reminder of the menorah in the Temple in Jerusalem.

Ark

- _____
- _____
- _____

Ner tamid

- _____
- _____
- _____

Bimah

- _____
- _____
- _____

Chapter 2: **Judaism: Practices**

Exam practice

Now answer the following exam question.

Name **two** of the internal features of a synagogue.

[2 marks]

1 _____

_____

2 _____

_____

> **TIP**
> It is OK to give one or two-word answers here – you don't need to spend time writing in full sentences.

Activity 2.3: Worship in Orthodox and Reform synagogues   pages 238–239

A Tick the boxes to show whether you think the following statements are most likely to be true of worship in an Orthodox synagogue or in a Reform synagogue.

	Orthodox	Reform
Emphasises the importance of obeying the Torah and Talmud.	☐	☐
Emphasises the importance of individual choice in worship.	☐	☐
Services are in Hebrew.	☐	☐
Men and women sit separately in services.	☐	☐
Women can perform all roles, including being a rabbi.	☐	☐
In the UK, services are in Hebrew and English.	☐	☐
Men and women sit together in services.	☐	☐
All rabbis are male.	☐	☐
There are different roles and religious duties for men and women.	☐	☐

B Use the space below to explain why Orthodox Judaism is considered to be more traditional than Reform Judaism. Try to give at least **two** different reasons.

_____

_____

_____

_____

_____

_____

_____

> **TIP**
> Orthodox Judaism and Reform Judaism are the two main branches of Judaism in the UK. Although they share many core beliefs, there are also differences in how they view and practise the Jewish faith. Referring to these similarities and differences will help you to write about contrasting views in the exam.

25

Chapter 2: **Judaism: Practices**

Activity 2.4: Daily services and prayer

 pages 240–241

Fill in the gaps in the sentences below using the words provided. (There are more words than gaps – you will have to decide which ones to leave out.)

Cairo   Amidah   beads   forehead   bimah   scripture   Reform   leg
Jerusalem   minyan   tallit   siddur   Orthodox   tefillin   mezuzah

Devout _____ Jews pray three times a day. Formal services in Orthodox synagogues are held in the morning, afternoon and evening. A _____ (a minimum of ten people) must be present for synagogue services. Daily prayers are taken from a book called a _____.

During morning prayers, Orthodox men wear a tallit, and on weekdays they also wear tefillin. In the Reform tradition, some men and women wear them too. The _____ is a shawl with a long tassel at each corner. The _____ are black leather boxes containing _____. One is fastened round the _____ and the other round the upper arm in line with the heart.

The _____ is also called the standing prayer. It is in all Jewish prayer services and is prayed while standing and facing _____. It includes blessings to praise God, blessings which are requests for God's help, and blessings to thank God.

Exam practice

Now answer the exam question below.

Which **one** of the following is known as the standing prayer? **[1 mark]**

Put a tick (✓) in the box next to the correct answer.

A The Aleinu ☐

B The Amidah ☐

C The Torah ☐

D The Shema ☐

Chapter 2: **Judaism: Practices**

Sources of religious belief and teaching

page 240

A Learn the following quotation about tefillin.

" And this shall serve you as a sign on your hand and as a reminder on your forehead – in order that the Teaching of the Lord may be in your mouth "
Exodus 13:9

This quotation from Exodus is the command that Jews are following when they wear tefillin. It explains that the tefillin are a visual reminder that faithful Jews should be talking about the Torah and passing on its teachings to their children.

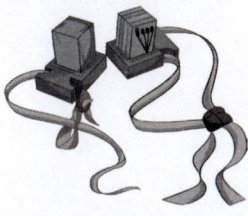

Fill in the gaps below. It will help you to learn the quotation if you say the whole thing out loud every time you write it.

" And this shall serve you as a _____ on your hand and as a reminder on your _____ – in order that the _____ of the Lord may be in your _____ "

Now cover up the text above and have a go at writing out the whole quotation from memory.

" _____
_____
_____ "

B Answer the following questions.

1. How do Jews wear tefillin?
   _____
   _____

2. Do you think that by wearing tefillin in this way, Jews are following the instructions in the quotation above? Explain your answer.
   _____
   _____
   _____

3. Why do Jews wear tefillin?
   _____
   _____
   _____

Chapter 2: **Judaism: Practices**

Activity 2.5: Shabbat in the synagogue

pages 242–243

Mark the following statements about Shabbat as true or false.

	True	False
Shabbat is celebrated on Sundays.	☐	☐
Shabbat is a day of rest.	☐	☐
Shabbat is a time to worship God and enjoy family life.	☐	☐
Celebrating Shabbat reminds Jews of the covenant made between God and Abraham.	☐	☐
There is a brief service in the synagogue on Friday evening.	☐	☐
The Torah is left in the Ark for the whole of Shabbat.	☐	☐

Sources of religious belief and teaching

page 242

A Learn the following quotation about Shabbat.

> "Remember the Sabbath day and keep it holy."
> *Exodus* 20:8

This quotation is from the Ten Commandments. It shows that by celebrating Shabbat, Jews are following a command from God.

Fill in the gaps below. It will help you to learn the quotation if you say the whole thing out loud every time you write it.

"_____ the _____ day and _____ it _____."

Now cover up the text above and have a go at writing out the whole quotation from memory.

"_____"

B Now answer this question.

1. What do Jews do to follow this commandment?

_____
_____
_____
_____

Chapter 2: **Judaism: Practices**

Activity 2.6: Shabbat in the home

pages 244–245

Answer these questions in sentences.

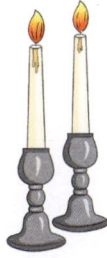

1. Who lights the Shabbat candles?

   _____
   _____
   _____

> **TIP**
> It is good to practise writing in full sentences because you will be expected to do this in the 4-, 5- and 12-mark questions in your exam. Try to use the correct religious terms in your answers.

2. What is the Kiddush cup used for?

   _____
   _____
   _____
   _____

3. What special food is often eaten as part of the Shabbat meal?

   _____
   _____
   _____
   _____

4. What Shabbat activities usually happen on Saturday?

   _____
   _____
   _____
   _____

5. What happens in the ceremony to mark the end of Shabbat?

   _____
   _____
   _____
   _____

Chapter 2: **Judaism: Practices**

Exam practice

Use your answers to the previous two activities to help you answer this exam question.

Explain **two** ways that Jews celebrate Shabbat.

Refer to scripture or another source of Jewish belief and teaching in your answer. **[5 marks]**

___

Activity 2.7: Worship in the home; the written and oral law

pages 246–247

Tick the correct answer for each of the questions below.

1. What is a mezuzah?

   ☐ A prayer shawl   ☐ A small box containing verses from the Torah fixed to a doorpost

   ☐ A special loaf eaten on Shabbat   ☐ A light in front of the Ark in the synagogue

2. Which of the following is **not** part of the Tenakh (the Jewish scriptures)?

   ☐ Torah   ☐ Nevi'im

   ☐ Gospels   ☐ Ketuvim

3. What is the Torah?

   ☐ The five books revealed to Moses   ☐ A book of psalms

   ☐ A commentary on the Mishnah   ☐ Part of the Talmud

4. What is the Talmud?

   ☐ The writings of the prophets   ☐ A book of prayers

   ☐ A book of psalms   ☐ A commentary on the Torah

Chapter 2: **Judaism: Practices**

Activity 2.8: The importance of the Torah and Talmud

pages 246–247

Read the statements below about what Jews should study to learn about their faith.

✓ Tick the box next to the statement if you think it could be used to support the argument that Jews should only study the Torah and Talmud.

✗ Put a cross in the box if you think it could be used to oppose the argument that Jews should only study the Torah and Talmud.

For each one, write a sentence deciding whether it could be used to support or oppose the argument that Jews should only study the Torah and Talmud.

[✓] The Torah was revealed to Moses by God. *The Torah is God's word, so Jews should pay attention to it. They need to study God's word if they want to learn about God and know how to please God.*

[ ] There are other parts to the Tenakh. _____

[ ] The Torah and Talmud were written thousands of years ago. _____

[ ] Synagogues provide classes and lectures about the faith. _____

[ ] The Talmud was written by rabbis to help Jews interpret the Torah. _____

[ ] Individual choice is important in worship. _____

Chapter 2: Judaism: Practices

Exam practice

Use your answers to Activity 2.8 to write a complete answer to this exam question.

'Jews should only seek guidance about their faith from the Torah and Talmud.'

Evaluate this statement. In your answer you should:
- give reasoned arguments to support this statement
- give reasoned arguments to support a different point of view
- refer to Jewish teaching
- reach a justified conclusion.

[12 marks]
[+3 SPaG marks]

REMEMBER...

Focus your answer on the statement you are asked to evaluate.

- Try to write at least three paragraphs – one with arguments to support the statement, one with arguments to support a different point of view, and a final paragraph with a justified conclusion stating which side you think is more convincing, and why.
- Look at the bullet points in the question, and make sure you include everything that they ask for.
- The key skill that you need to demonstrate is evaluation. This means expressing judgements on the arguments that support or oppose the statement, based on evidence. You might decide an argument is strong because it is based on a source of religious belief and teaching, such as a teaching from the Tenakh, or because it is based on scientific evidence. You might decide an argument is weak because it is based on a personal opinion, or a popular idea with no formal evidence. You can use phrases in your chains of reasoning such as 'I think this a convincing argument because…' or 'In my opinion, this is a weak argument because…'.

Chapter 2: **Judaism: Practices**

Activity 2.9: Ceremonies associated with birth pages 248–249

The following statements are muddled up. Copy them out into the correct boxes below to show which ceremony they relate to.

- For girls, this traditionally happens in the synagogue
- When some Orthodox Jews give a small amount of money
- When a baby boy is circumcised
- Formally introduces the baby to the community and to God
- Happens at eight days old
- 'Redeems' the firstborn son from Temple service
- Happens 31 days after birth
- The baby is placed on a chair that symbolises the presence of the prophet Elijah
- Keeps the covenant with Abraham

Naming ceremony	
Brit Milah	
Redemption of the First Born Son	

Chapter 2: **Judaism: Practices**

Activity 2.10: Bar and Bat Mitzvah

 pages 250–251

Fill in the gaps in the sentences below about Bar and Bat Mitzvah.

Jewish young people take part in a ceremony when they are considered old enough to take responsibility for practising their f_____. This happens at the age of t_____ for a boy and the age of t_____ for a girl.

The ceremony is called B_____ for a boy, and Reform Jews may hold a B_____ for a girl.

There are often classes at the s_____ to prepare for the event. This preparation brings Jews closer to G_____. During the ceremony, the young person will read from the T_____ in the synagogue, and may wear a t_____ for the first time. There will often be a meal or p_____ following the service.

The ceremony is when a Jew is seen to become an adult, and is when they are allowed to become part of a m_____.

Exam practice

Now answer this exam question.

Explain **two** reasons why Bar Mitzvah and Bat Mitzvah are important ceremonies in Judaism. **[4 marks]**

_____
_____
_____
_____
_____
_____
_____
_____
_____
_____

35

Chapter 2: **Judaism: Practices**

Activity 2.11: Marriage pages 252–253

Answer the following questions about Jewish marriage in sentences.

1. What is the betrothal?

2. What is a ketubah, and what might it include?

3. What does the chuppah symbolise?

4. Why might a Jewish couple fast on their wedding day?

5. How many wedding blessings are recited after the marriage contract is signed?

6. What does breaking the glass represent?

7. Why is marriage important to Jews?

Chapter 2: **Judaism: Practices**.

Activity 2.12: Mourning for the dead

pages 254–255

The following statements describe different periods of mourning after the death of a loved one. They have been muddled up. Copy them into the correct boxes below.

- Mourners say a blessing referring to God as the true judge
- Ends with a meal of condolence made up of bread and eggs
- Male mourners say the kaddish daily in the synagogue
- Mourners stay at home and hold prayer services three times a day
- Mourners make a small tear in their clothes
- Children continue to say the kaddish for a parent who has died
- Close family are left to grieve without having to follow all the Jewish laws
- An intense period of mourning starting on the day of the burial
- Lasts until 30 days after the person's death
- Lasts for 11 months, during which time mourners do not attend parties

When the death is announced	• •
The first period of mourning	• •
The second period of mourning (shiva)	• •
The lesser period of mourning	• •
The final period of mourning	• •

Chapter 2: **Judaism: Practices**

Activity 2.13: Dietary laws

pages 256–257

A Tick the boxes to show whether these foods are kosher (allowed for Jews according to the food laws in the Torah) or trefah (not allowed for Jews according to the food laws in the Torah).

	Kosher	Trefah
Dairy and meat together	☐	☐
Pork	☐	☐
An animal that has been killed with a very sharp knife by a Jewish butcher	☐	☐
Salmon	☐	☐
An animal that has been stunned unconscious before it is killed	☐	☐
Strawberries that are free of insects	☐	☐

B Now answer the following questions.

1. Write down **two** ways that a Jewish person might make sure their food is kosher.

   1 _____
   _____

   2 _____
   _____

2. Give **one** reason why Orthodox Jews follow the dietary laws strictly.
   _____
   _____

3. Give **one** reason why many Reform Jews don't follow the dietary laws strictly.
   _____
   _____

Key terms

pages 236–259

A These terms and their meanings are muddled up. Write out the meanings in the correct order in the second table on the next page.

Aron Hakodesh	A prayer shawl
Brit Milah	The holiest part of the synagogue where the Torah scrolls are kept
Kosher	A small box which contains verses from the Torah and is fixed to a doorpost
Tallit	The holiest and most important day in the Jewish calendar
Mezuzah	A ceremony of male circumcision
Yom Kippur	Food that is acceptable to eat according to Jewish dietary laws

Chapter 2: **Judaism: Practices**

Aron Hakodesh	
Brit Milah	
Kosher	
Tallit	
Mezuzah	
Yom Kippur	

B Now write the correct term beside each meaning. For an extra challenge, cover up the rest of this activity and try to see if you can recall the words from memory.

A small box which contains verses from the Torah and is fixed to a doorpost	
The holiest and most important day in the Jewish calendar	
A prayer shawl	
Food that is acceptable to eat according to the Jewish dietary laws	
A ceremony of male circumcision	
The holiest part of the synagogue where the Torah scrolls are kept	

Chapter 2: **Judaism: Practices**

Activity 2.14: Rosh Hashanah and Yom Kippur

pages 258–259

Tick the boxes to show whether these statements refer to Yom Kippur or Rosh Hashanah.

Statement	Yom Kippur	Rosh Hashanah
Celebrates the start of the Jewish new year.	☐	☐
Jews focus on asking God to forgive their sins.	☐	☐
The anniversary of the day on which God created humans.	☐	☐
The most holy and important day in the year for Jews.	☐	☐
Jews fast (do not eat or drink) for 25 hours.	☐	☐
A ram's horn (shofar) is blown 100 times in the synagogue.	☐	☐
White clothes are worn as a symbol of purity.	☐	☐
The evening before, families share a festive meal together.	☐	☐

Activity 2.15: Foods eaten at Pesach

pages 260–261

Pesach is a festival that remembers the Jews' escape from Egypt, where they were working as slaves. Some of the food and drink that is consumed during Pesach reminds Jews of their escape from Egypt in different ways.

Complete this table to describe the foods eaten at Pesach and what they represent.

Food or drink	How does it remind Jews of their escape from Egypt?
Red wine	

40

Chapter 2: **Judaism: Practices**

_____	Recalls how the Jews did not have time to let their bread rise before they fled from Egypt. Eating this fulfils a command from God that helps to remember the escape from Egypt (Exodus 12:15).
Green vegetable dipped in salt water	The green vegetable may symbolise... The salt water represents...
_____	Bitter herbs represent... The charoset is made of... It symbolises... It reminds Jews that...
Roasted egg and _____	

41

Chapter 2: Judaism: Practices

Key Terms Glossary

As you progress through the course, you can collect the meanings of useful terms in the glossary below. You can then use the completed glossaries to revise from.

To do well in the exam you will need to understand these terms and include them in your answers. Tick the shaded circles to record how confident you feel.

- ○ I recognise this term
- ○ I understand what this term means
- ○ I can use this term in a sentence

Amidah

Ark (Aron Hakodesh)

Bar Mitzvah

Bat Mitzvah

Bimah

Brit Milah

Dietary laws

Kaddish

Kosher

Marriage ceremony

Minyan

Chapter 2: **Judaism: Practices**

Mourning rituals

Ner tamid

Pesach

Rosh Hashanah

Shabbat

Shiva

Synagogue

Tallit

Talmud

Tefillin

Trefah

Yom Kippur

43

Chapter 3: Exam practice: Judaism

Test the 1-mark question

Example

1 Which **one** of the following terms best expresses the meaning of the word Shekhinah? **[1 mark]**

   Put a tick (✓) in the box next to the correct answer.

   A Judgement ☐

   B Covenant ☐

   C Divine presence ✓

   D Justice ☐ ✓ (1)

WHAT WILL THE QUESTION LOOK LIKE?

The 1-mark question will always be a **multiple-choice question** with four answers to choose from. Only one answer is correct. The question will usually start with the words **'Which one of the following…'**.

HOW IS IT MARKED?

You will receive 1 mark for choosing the correct answer.

! REMEMBER…

Read the question carefully before making your choice. Even if you are not sure of the right answer, make a guess – you may get it right anyway.

Be aware that if you tick more than one box, you will receive no marks, even if one of your selected answers is correct.

Activity

2 Which **one** of the following stages of life is associated with Brit Milah? **[1 mark]**

   Put a tick (✓) in the box next to the correct answer.

   A Birth ☐

   B Coming of age ☐

   C Marriage ☐

   D Death ☐

3 Which **one** of the following is a reading platform in a synagogue? **[1 mark]**

   Put a tick (✓) in the box next to the correct answer.

   A Aron Hakodesh ☐

   B Ner tamid ☐

   C Amidah ☐

   D Bimah ☐

Chapter 3: **Exam practice: Judaism**

Test the 2-mark question

Example

1 Give **two** items of food that according to Jewish dietary laws cannot be eaten together. **[2 marks]**

1 *Meat.* ✓ (1)

2 *Milk.* ✓ (1)

WHAT WILL THE QUESTION LOOK LIKE?

The 2-mark question will always start with the words **'Give two…'** or **'Name two…'**, and a maximum of **2 marks** will be awarded.

HOW IS IT MARKED?

The examiner is looking for two different, correct answers. For each correct response you will receive 1 mark.

! REMEMBER…

You need to give **two pieces of information** in your answer. Use the numbered lines to make sure you write two separate points. Don't just repeat yourself – make each point say something new.

Keep your answers short. You only need to provide two facts or short ideas; **you don't need to explain them or express any opinions**.

TIP

For 2-mark questions like this one, it is OK to write your answers as single words if that is all that is necessary. You don't need to spend time writing in complete sentences.

Activity

2 Give **two** Jewish beliefs about the nature of God. **[2 marks]**

The sample answer below would get 1 mark because only one correct answer is given. Add another Jewish belief about the nature of God to make the answer worth 2 marks.

1 *God is loving.* ✓ (1)

2 _____

3 Give **two** Jewish key moral principles. **[2 marks]**

1 _____

2 _____

4 Give **two** promises God made to Abraham when he told him to go 'to the land that I will show you' (*Genesis* 12:1). **[2 marks]**

1 _____

2 _____

Chapter 3: **Exam practice: Judaism**

Test the 4-mark question

Example

1. Explain **two** ways in which the mitzvot between man and God influence Jews today. **[4 marks]**

One way in which the mitzvot between man and God influence Jews today is that Jews follow the first four commandments, ✓(1) such as not worshipping any other gods because God is one. ✓(1)

Jews will also keep the Shabbat as a day devoted to God. ✓(1) They do this by resting and attending worship in the synagogue. ✓(1)

! REMEMBER...

Make **two different points**. Try to show the examiner where each point begins. For example, you could start your answer with 'One way is…' and then move on to your second point by saying something like 'Another way is…' or 'Jews will also…'.

Try to **add detail** to each point, by giving an example or adding more explanation. Adding detail to your points in this way will earn you more marks.

WHAT WILL THE QUESTION LOOK LIKE?

The 4-mark question will always start with the words **'Explain two…'**, and a maximum of **4 marks** will be awarded. You are asked to 'Explain', which means you need to show extra detail in both of your points for full marks.

HOW IS IT MARKED?

This answer would gain 4 marks because it makes two different points, and both points clearly show extra detail.

THE 'GREAT BRITAIN' QUESTION

You may have to answer a question which refers to Judaism and the main religious tradition of Great Britain. **The main religious tradition of Great Britain is Christianity, and you must refer to Christianity in your answer.** You may be asked to compare the two religions by writing about similarities or contrasts (differences) on two topics, monotheism and God as creator, and contrasting beliefs about the Messiah.

Activity

2. Explain **two** contrasting ways worship is carried out in a synagogue. **[4 marks]**

The sample answer below would get 4 marks because there are two points that show two contrasting (different) ways of worshipping in a synagogue, and each point has extra detail. Add a tick next to each point. Then underline the extra detail that has been added to each point.

In Orthodox synagogues, services are conducted in Hebrew. This is the original language of the Jews.

In Reform synagogues in Britain and America, English is also used for the services. This is so worshippers can understand the services more easily.

TIP

Sometimes a question may ask you to explain two **contrasting** beliefs/ways, etc. This means your second point must provide a contrast to your first point (i.e. show a difference).

Chapter 3: **Exam practice: Judaism**

3 Explain **two** ways in which religious beliefs about God as creator are similar in Judaism and in the main religious tradition of Great Britain.

You should name the main religious tradition of Great Britain in your answer. **[4 marks]**

The sample answer below would get 2 marks because it makes one point and then adds extra detail to this point. It includes reference to both Judaism and Christianity. Add a second point for a third mark. If you can add detail to that point with an appropriate example or more explanation, the complete answer will get 4 marks.

TIP
Here is an example of the 'Great Britain' question. See the text on page 46 for guidance.

One way in which Jewish and Christian beliefs are similar is that they both believe God created people as his final act of creation. ✓(1) The man Adam was first, followed by the first woman who was called Eve. ✓(1)

A second way... _____
_____
_____
_____

4 Explain **two** ways that the dietary laws influence Jews today. **[4 marks]**

The sample answer below would get 2 marks for giving two different ways. Add detail to each point to gain 2 more marks.

One way is that Jews need to buy meat from a Kosher butcher. ✓(1)
_____
_____
_____
_____

A second way is that Jews may choose to have two separate kitchens or food preparation areas. ✓(1)
_____
_____
_____
_____

TIP
It is a good idea to start your second point on a new line, to make it clear where it begins.

47

Chapter 3: **Exam practice: Judaism**

5 Explain **two** contrasting Jewish beliefs about life after death. [4 marks]

6 Explain **two** ways that the belief about saving life (pikuach nefesh) influences Jews today. [4 marks]

Make one point → Develop it

Make a second point → Develop it

48

Chapter 3: **Exam practice: Judaism**

Test the 5-mark question

Example

1. Explain **two** Jewish beliefs about Shabbat.

   Refer to scripture or another source of Jewish belief and teaching in your answer. **[5 marks]**

   One Jewish belief about Shabbat is that it must be a day devoted to God. ✓ (1) *For example, Jewish families are encouraged to attend synagogue on Saturday morning in order to worship God.* ✓ (1)

   A second belief is that Shabbat should be a day of rest. ✓ (1) *It says in Exodus that you can work for six days but on the seventh you must rest and not work.* ✓ (1) *For example, on Shabbat, Orthodox Jews will not cook food or drive cars.* ✓ (1)

> **WHAT WILL THE QUESTION LOOK LIKE?**
>
> The 5-mark question will always start with the words **'Explain two…'** and end with the words **'Refer to scripture or another source of Jewish belief and teaching in your answer'**. A maximum of **5 marks** will be awarded.

> **HOW IS IT MARKED?**
>
> This answer would gain 5 marks because it makes two different points, and both points have extra detail. It also refers to a relevant source of Jewish belief and teaching.

! REMEMBER...

The 5-mark question is similar to the 4-mark question, so try to make **two different points** and **add extra detail** to each of them.

The additional instruction in the question asks you to **'refer to scripture or another source of Jewish belief and teaching in your answer'**. Try to think of a reference to the Tenakh or Talmud, the words of a Jewish prayer, or a quotation from a Jewish leader (such as a well-known rabbi) to back up one of your points. You only need one reference but can add more than one if you want.

Activity

2. Explain **two** Jewish beliefs about the role of Moses in the Sinai covenant.

   Refer to scripture or another source of Jewish belief and teaching in your answer. **[5 marks]**

   The sample answer below would get 5 marks because there are two points with extra detail, and a reference to a source of belief and teaching. Add a tick next to each point. Then underline where each point has extra detail. Finally, draw a circle around a reference to scripture or a Jewish belief and teaching.

   The first belief is that Moses became the leader of the Jews on their journey to Sinai and the Promised Land. He trusted that God would keep him safe because he was doing God's work.

   The second belief is that Moses received the Ten Commandments from God on Mount Sinai and passed them on to the rest of the Jews so they could follow God's requirements, such as 'Thou shall not murder.'

49

Chapter 3: **Exam practice: Judaism**

3 Explain **two** Jewish beliefs about life after death.

Refer to scripture or another source of Jewish belief and teaching in your answer. **[5 marks]**

> The sample answer below would get 4 marks as there is one point with extra detail, and one simple point. There is no reference to scripture or another source of Jewish belief and teaching. Try to gain the maximum of 5 marks by adding detail to the second point, and adding a source of Jewish belief and teaching to either of the points – it doesn't matter which.

Firstly, Jews believe that they will go to Gan Eden or paradise when they die. ✓ **(1)**
To achieve this, they have to follow their faith correctly. ✓ **(1)**

Secondly, some Jews think that when they die, they are judged by God. ✓ **(1)**

TIP
You don't need to quote a source of belief and teaching word for word, but try to say where it came from. For example, whether it came from the Tenakh, a Jewish prayer, a speech by a well-known rabbi, etc.

4 Explain **two** ways Jews use the Tenakh in their daily life.

Refer to scripture or another source of Jewish belief and teaching in your answer. **[5 marks]**

> The sample answer below would get 2 marks as there is one point with extra detail. Complete the answer by adding a second point with extra detail, as well as a reference to a source of Jewish belief and teaching (this can be added to either point).

Orthodox Jews carefully study the Tenakh ✓ **(1)** *in order to help them to make important decisions in their life correctly.* ✓ **(1)**

TIP
Here, your source of Jewish belief and teaching is likely to be from the Tenakh itself.

Chapter 3: **Exam practice: Judaism**

5 Explain **two** Jewish beliefs about free will.
Refer to scripture or another source of Jewish belief and teaching in your answer. **[5 marks]**

_____
_____
_____
_____
_____
_____
_____
_____
_____
_____
_____
_____

6 Explain **two** Jewish beliefs about the origins of Pesach.
Refer to scripture or another source of Jewish belief and teaching in your answer. **[5 marks]**

_____
_____
_____
_____
_____
_____
_____
_____
_____
_____
_____
_____

Chapter 3: **Exam practice: Judaism**

Test the 12-mark question

Example

1 'For Jews, the Amidah (standing prayer) is the most important prayer.'

Evaluate this statement.

In your answer you should:
- give reasoned arguments to support this statement
- give reasoned arguments to support a different point of view
- refer to Jewish teaching
- reach a justified conclusion.

[12 marks]
[+3 SPaG marks]

WHAT WILL THE QUESTION LOOK LIKE?

The 12-mark question will always ask you to **evaluate** a statement. The bullet points underneath the statement will tell you the things the examiner expects to see in your answer. Here, you need to give reasoned arguments for and against the statement, and refer to Jewish teaching. The final bullet will always ask you to 'reach a justified conclusion'.

HOW IS IT MARKED?

The examiner will mark your answer using level descriptors (see below).

In addition, 3 extra marks will be awarded for your **spelling, punctuation and grammar** (SPaG), and your use of **specialist terminology**. This applies to both of the 12-mark questions that you answer on the Judaism paper.

> **! REMEMBER...**
>
> **Evaluating** means to make a judgement, using **evidence** to decide how convincing you find the statement to be.
>
> You should consider **arguments in support of the statement**, and decide how convincing you think those are, giving at least one chain of reasoning. You then need to consider **why some people might support a different point of view**, and decide how convincing they are, again giving at least one chain of reasoning.
>
> You might want to decide how convincing an argument is by considering where it comes from. Is it based on a source of Jewish belief and teaching, such as a teaching from a holy book, or something advised by a religious leader? If so, you may decide this evidence strengthens the argument and therefore whether you would support or oppose the statement in the question.
>
> You might decide an argument is weak because it is only a personal opinion, or a popular idea with no strong evidence to support it. This would make it difficult for you to use to support or oppose the statement in the question when reaching a judgement and you must **explain the reasons why you reach your judgements**.
>
> To reach a **justified conclusion** you should consider both sides of the argument, and make your own judgement about which you find more convincing. You might conclude that each side has its own strengths. To make sure your conclusion is 'justified', you need to give **reasons or evidence to support your view**, but don't *just* repeat all the reasons and evidence you have already used.

Level descriptors

Level	
Level 1 (1–3 marks)	• Point of view with reason(s) stated in support.
Level 2 (4–6 marks)	• Reasoned consideration of a point of view. • A logical chain of reasoning drawing on knowledge and understanding of relevant evidence and information. OR • Recognition of different points of view, each supported by relevant reasons/evidence. • **Maximum of Level 2 if there is no reference to religion.**
Level 3 (7–9 marks)	• Reasoned consideration of different points of view. • Logical chains of reasoning that draw on knowledge and understanding of relevant evidence and information. • **Clear reference to religion.**
Level 4 (10–12 marks)	• A well-argued response, reasoned consideration of different points of view. • Logical chains of reasoning leading to judgement(s) supported by knowledge and understanding of relevant evidence and information. • **Reference to religion applied to the issue.**

Chapter 3: **Exam practice: Judaism**

Logical chains of reasoning

The level descriptors state that to achieve the higher levels you need to show 'logical chains of reasoning' in your answer. This is not as difficult as it sounds. It simply refers to an argument where one idea connects logically to the next.

If you take an idea, develop it by giving more detail and explanation, then provide evidence that supports your idea, you will be demonstrating a logical chain of reasoning. Each step in your argument is a link: together they make a chain of reasoning.

This might already be part of your normal way of writing, even if the phrase is new to you.

You will find some examples in the sample answers that follow.

2 'Jews should obey all 613 mitzvot in the Torah.'

Evaluate this statement.

In your answer you should:

- give reasoned arguments to support this statement
- give reasoned arguments to support a different point of view
- refer to Jewish teaching
- reach a justified conclusion.

[12 marks]
[+3 SPaG marks]

Here are four sample answers to the question above. Each one would be awarded a different level. Read all four answers carefully and compare them with the level descriptors on page 52.

Level 1 sample answer

This is a Level 1 answer because:

- it expresses an opinion
- it gives a reason.

To improve this answer the student could:

- create a simple chain of reasoning by giving relevant examples
- include a different point of view with reasons.

I agree that all 613 mitzvot should be followed. My reason for this is that they were given to Moses by God so they must be important. They help Jews to live a good life.

TIP
Here the student mentions the origins of the mitzvot, with a mention of what they help Jews to do. Adding some examples of mitzvot that help Jews to live a good life would help to improve their answer.

Chapter 3: **Exam practice: Judaism**

Level 2 sample answer

This is a Level 2 answer because:
- it adds a little more reasoning and evidence
- it mentions a different point of view.

To improve this answer the student could:
- add more reasons
- use a logical chain of reasoning for each point of view.

I agree that all 613 mitzvot should be followed. My reason for this is that they were given to Moses by God so they must be important. They help Jews to live a good life by following the laws God has given, including following the Ten Commandments.

Some others say that although many of the mitzvot are very useful, there are some that are out of date and do not help.

TIP
Try to make your different point of view of similar length to your 'agree' paragraph. This has not happened here.

TIP
You might find it helps to structure your answer so all of the arguments to support the statement are grouped together, and all of the arguments to support a different view are grouped together – as the student has done here.

Level 3 sample answer

This is a Level 3 answer because:
- there is a reasoned consideration of different points of view
- it contains chains of reasoning
- it includes a justified conclusion.

To improve this answer the student could:
- provide more detail in the chains of reasoning
- develop the conclusion further.

I agree that all 613 mitzvot should be followed. My reason for this is that they were given to Moses by God so they must be important. They help Jews to live a good life by following the laws God has given, including following the Ten Commandments. Many mitzvot help people to have a good relationship with God. Some of them are about what Jews should and should not do on Shabbat, which helps them to know what work should and should not be done. This may help them to live in a way that will guarantee them a place in paradise.

Some other Jews say that although many of the mitzvot are very useful, there are some examples that are out of date and do not help. They were first written around 3,000 years ago when the way of life was very different from how it is now. Rules about dietary requirements are much harder to keep nowadays. For example, ready-made meals and products such as biscuits and cakes may have both meat and milk products in them and you don't know that they are not kosher.

My conclusion is that Jews should obey as many mitzvot as they can.

TIP
To write a Level 3 answer, you need to show 'clear reference to religion'. This can be achieved by using accurate religious terms (such as 'the Ten Commandments' and 'kosher'), and including clear beliefs about God or other aspects of a religion (such as the idea that the mitzvot come from God).

TIP
Here, the brief conclusion matches the view in the first paragraph. However, if once you've written your answer, you have changed your mind, you can include this in your conclusion together with at least one reason why. It can really help if you write down some notes to plan out your answer.

TIP
This conclusion is very brief. However, when justifying your conclusion, do not just repeat the reasons you have previously given. Try to think of something else.

Chapter 3: **Exam practice: Judaism**

Level 4 sample answer

This is a Level 4 answer because:
- it is well argued
- it contains extra points, reasons and evidence that build on the chains of reasoning in the Level 3 answer
- it includes a more reasoned, justified conclusion.

I agree that all 613 mitzvot should be followed if possible. My reason for this is that they were given to Moses by God so they must be important. They help Jews to live a good life by following the laws God has given, including following the Ten Commandments. Many mitzvot help people to have a good relationship with God. Some of them are about what Jews should and should not do on Shabbat, which helps them to know what work should and should not be done. This may help them to live in a way that will guarantee them a place in heaven, which is their main aim in life.

Some other Jews (such as some Reform Jews) say that although many of the mitzvot are very useful, there are some examples that are out of date and do not help. They were first written around 3,000 years ago when the way of life was very different from how it is now. Rules about dietary requirements are much harder to keep nowadays. For example, ready-made meals and products such as biscuits and cakes may have both meat and milk products in them and you don't know that they are not kosher. Also, the mitzvot about bringing sacrifices to the Temple are useless today because there is no Temple. In addition, Shabbat law can be broken in order to save a life, so life is more important than the mitzvot. This is called pikuach nefesh.

However, mitzvot are useful because they help Jews to exercise free will correctly, by guiding Jews into making good choices for themselves and the Jewish community. They can choose to do what they want but they know that if they choose to do something that breaks any of the mitzvot, they are not choosing to do what God wants them to do, which is not being respectful to him.

My conclusion is that even though in an ideal world Jews should obey all of the mitzvot, not all of them apply today, such as ones to do with sacrificing animals to God. Free will allows Jews to ignore the mitzvot that don't apply. This is different from breaking them. As God is the eternal creator and sustainer, it makes no sense to use the free will he gave people to break his rules.

TIP There is a lot of detail in the reasoning in this paragraph. The opinion, reason, further detail explanation and the conclusion makes it a logical chain of reasoning leading to a judgement. This helps to make it a well-argued response.

TIP This is a good paragraph because it clearly links the time when the mitzvot were first written with the present day.

TIP The student has used specific examples and religious teachings, such as references to kosher food, Temple sacrifices and free will.

TIP The student has written a justified conclusion, expressing a judgement and giving reasons for why they have reached that judgement. They refer back briefly to some of their earlier points which helps make this a good summary ending to the answer.

Chapter 3: **Exam practice: Judaism**

Activity

3 'Mourning rituals help Jews to remember the dead.'

Evaluate this statement.

In your answer you should:

- give reasoned arguments to support this statement
- give reasoned arguments to support a different point of view
- refer to Jewish teaching
- reach a justified conclusion.

[12 marks]
[+3 SPaG marks]

A Read the sample answer below.

The purpose of mourning rituals is to allow friends and family to remember the dead. There is a system of mourning that Jews follow which is well set out. It starts with a funeral that is usually in a graveyard, which is a place of the dead not the living. This means that everybody attending the funeral knows where the body is buried so they can visit when they want. Jewish law requires a gravestone to be placed on the grave so it can be remembered.

Mourning lasts for a year. When the death is announced, following the example of Jacob in Genesis, close family members make a small tear in their clothes and say a blessing. The small tear helps them to remember as it is never mended. An intense period of mourning called shiva lasts for seven days from the day of the burial. During this time, Jews don't work but stay at home where they hold prayer services. These services focus on the person who has died and help Jews to remember them. I think this is a very important way of remembering. But other practices during this time, such as Jews not focusing on their appearance, don't seem to me to help them to remember. Nor does the next period of 30 days when normal life resumes (apart from them not cutting their hair or enjoying themselves). I think that saying the kaddish every day does help them to keep their deceased family member in their mind though.

Some would say that the funeral rituals focus on the person who is dead, not on the person who they knew when they were alive (the person they want to remember), so the funeral ritual is not helpful as a way of remembering.

There are a lot of mourning rituals which all have meaning. Some of these directly help Jews to remember the person who has died, but there is also a strong focus on God. People are encouraged to visit graveyards and often place a small stone on the gravestone to show they have visited. People respond differently to death, but importantly the mourning rituals help Jews to not only remember the person who has died but to remember God as well.

Chapter 3: **Exam practice: Judaism**

B Now answer the following questions about the sample answer above.

1. Write down **two** of the arguments used to support the statement.

2. Summarise the argument made against the statement.

3. Do you think the example about making a small tear in their clothes is a good one? Why or why not?

4. Which of the arguments do you think is strongest? Why?

5. The question says you should 'refer to Jewish teachings'. Using a coloured pen, highlight any references to Jewish teaching that you can find.

    Underline any part where the student gives a personal judgement.

6. 'The question asks you to reach a 'justified conclusion'. Do you think the last paragraph is a good 'justified conclusion'? Explain your answer.

Chapter 3: **Exam practice: Judaism**

4 'Celebrating Shabbat at home is more important than celebrating it in a synagogue.'

Evaluate this statement.

In your answer you should:

- give reasoned arguments to support this statement
- give reasoned arguments to support a different point of view
- refer to Jewish teaching
- reach a justified conclusion.

[12 marks]
[+3 SPaG marks]

The answer below is a Level 1 answer because it gives a point of view and has a couple of simple reasons to support it. In the space below, turn this into a Level 2 answer. You could do this by either:

- explaining further the idea of a family getting together to show their love for God and each other by eating a special meal. Try to do this in such a way as to turn what the student has written into a 'logical chain of reasoning'

or:

- adding a different point of view, with a simple reason to support it.

I agree that celebrating Shabbat at home is more important than celebrating it in a synagogue because it is an opportunity for Jewish families to have time together and to eat a special meal every Friday night.

Chapter 3: **Exam practice: Judaism**

Now rewrite your answer so it is likely to achieve at least Level 3. To do this, you should:

- provide more reasons and evidence to support the statement. For example, you could focus on the fact that Shabbat is a day of rest (rather than a day of worship and prayers)
- make a reasoned argument for the importance of celebrating Shabbat in a synagogue
- include a clear reference to religion. For example, you could include some facts about what happens during Shabbat worship at home and/or in the synagogue, to support your arguments for and/or against the statement
- attempt to write a conclusion, possibly by making the reasoned point that both are important.

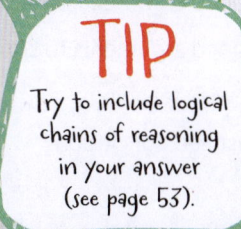

TIP
Try to include logical chains of reasoning in your answer (see page 53).

Chapter 3: **Exam practice: Judaism**

5 'The Jewish dietary laws should be relaxed because they are too difficult to follow.'

Evaluate this statement.

In your answer you should:

- give reasoned arguments to support this statement
- give reasoned arguments to support a different point of view
- refer to Jewish teaching
- reach a justified conclusion.

[12 marks]
[+3 SPaG marks]

> **! REMEMBER…**
>
> Focus your answer on the statement you are asked to evaluate.
>
> - Try to write at least three paragraphs – one with arguments to support the statement, one with arguments to support a different point of view, and a final paragraph with a justified conclusion stating which side you think is more convincing, and why.
> - Look at the bullet points in the question, and make sure you include everything that they ask for.
> - The key skill that you need to demonstrate is evaluation. This means expressing judgements on the arguments that support or oppose the statement, based on evidence. You might decide an argument is strong because it is based on a source of religious belief and teaching, such as a teaching from the Tenakh, or because it is based on scientific evidence. You might decide an argument is weak because it is based on a personal opinion, or a popular idea with no formal evidence. You can use phrases in your chain of reasoning such as 'I think this a convincing argument because…' or 'In my opinion, this is a weak argument because…'.

Chapter 4: Theme A: Religion, relationships and ethical studies

Activity 4.1: Human beings as sexual, male and female
pages 264–265

A Answer these questions in sentences.

1. In Genesis, God tells Adam and Eve to 'be fruitful and multiply'. What does this teach Christians about the purpose of sex?
   _____
   _____

2. Why does the Catholic Church teach that sex should not take place between a couple until they are married?
   _____
   _____
   _____
   _____

3. Give **two** reasons why the Catholic Church is against adultery.

   1 _____
   _____

   2 _____
   _____

B The Catholic Church teaches that sex should be marital, procreative and unitive. According to this teaching, which of the following statements are true or false? Tick the correct box for each one.

	True	False
It is acceptable for a Catholic couple to regularly use contraception.	☐	☐
Sex should bring a couple closer to each other.	☐	☐
Sex before marriage is approved by the Catholic Church.	☐	☐
Casual sex with more than one partner is OK.	☐	☐
Sex should be open to creating new life.	☐	☐

Chapter 4: **Theme A: Religion, relationships and ethical studies**

Activity 4.2: Pope John Paul II's 'Theology of the Body'

pages 266–267

A Tick the statements below if you think they are ideas presented by John Paul II in his 'Theology of the Body' talks.

God loves every human being for their own sake. ☐

Men are more important than women. ☐

Sex is not an important part of marriage. ☐

Sex is an expression of mutual love and respect. ☐

Extramarital sex is not acceptable. ☐

Couples should have as many children as they want. ☐

B Now correct any statements that you do not think are ideas included in the 'Theology of the Body', so they do match its teaching.

_____
_____
_____
_____
_____
_____
_____

Exam practice

Now answer the following exam question.

Give **two** teachings from John Paul II's 'Theology of the Body'. **[2 marks]**

1 _____
_____

2 _____
_____

TIP
Remember that for the 2-mark question you just need to make two simple points – you don't need to explain the teachings or say what they mean.

63

Chapter 4: **Theme A: Religion, relationships and ethical studies**

Activity 4.3: Human sexuality and its expression

pages 268–269

Fill in the table below to give different views in Britain on sex and marriage.

TIP

It is useful to be able to give an opposing point of view, even if you don't agree with it. For example, you might agree that adultery is always wrong, but try to think of at least one reason why a Humanist might disagree with you.

	The Catholic Church	Other Christian Churches	Non-religious views (e.g. Humanist views)
Sex before marriage		Teach that sexual relationships should wait until marriage, but accept that some Christian couples do have sex before marriage.	
Adultery	Teaches that adultery is wrong. This is because it breaks the marriage promises made before God, and is a betrayal of trust.		
Same-sex relationships			Humanists accept same-sex relationships and agree with the legalisation of same-sex marriage.

Chapter 4: Theme A: Religion, relationships and ethical studies

Exam practice

Now answer the exam question below.

Which **one** of the following refers to sex outside marriage? [1 mark]

Put a tick (✓) in the box next to the correct answer.

A Contraception ☐   B Adultery ☐   C Nuptial ☐   D Divorce ☐

Activity 4.4: A valid marriage in the Catholic Church

pages 270–271

Which of the following are conditions for a valid marriage in the Catholic Church? Mark the statements as true if you think they are a condition, or false if you think they are not a condition.

	True	False
The couple must be free to marry.	☐	☐
One of the couple can be married to someone else already.	☐	☐
The couple must be getting married out of their own free will.	☐	☐
The couple must not be closely related (e.g. first cousins or siblings).	☐	☐
The marriage must be made in the presence of a Catholic bishop.	☐	☐
The couple must declare that they are willing to accept children lovingly from God.	☐	☐
The marriage is not valid until the couple have kissed each other.	☐	☐

Sources of religious belief and teaching

page 272

A Learn the following quotation.

> ❝to have and to hold from this day forward, for better for worse, for richer for poorer, in sickness and in health, to love and to cherish, till death do us part.❞

This quotation is from the marriage promises that Catholic couples make to each other.

Fill in the gaps below. It will help you to learn the quotation if you say the whole thing out loud every time you write it.

❝to have and to _____ from this day _____, for better for

_____, for richer for _____, in sickness and in

_____, to love and to _____, till _____

do us part.❞

Chapter 4: **Theme A: Religion, relationships and ethical studies**

Now have a go at writing out the whole quotation from memory.

"_____

_____

_____ "

B Now answer the following questions.

1. Which part of this quotation shows that marriage is intended to be lifelong?
_____
_____

2. Does this quotation teach Catholics that a married couple should stay committed to each other even when bad things are happening in their lives? Explain your answer.
_____
_____
_____

Activity 4.5: Cohabitation

page 273

Answer these questions in sentences.

1. What does 'cohabitation' mean?
_____
_____

2. Give **two** reasons why the Catholic Church disagrees with cohabitation.

1 _____
_____

2 _____
_____

3. Give **two** reasons why a couple might decide to cohabit.

1 _____
_____

2 _____
_____

Chapter 4: Theme A: Religion, relationships and ethical studies

Activity 4.6: Annulment, divorce and remarriage

pages 274–275

A Fill in the gaps in the sentences below using the words provided. (There are more words than gaps – you will have to decide which ones to leave out.)

sex	epistle	idolatry	annulment	the Pope	remarried
Communion		children	divorce		remarriage
death	adultery	God	marriage	died	contraception

_____ is a statement from the Catholic Church that a marriage was not valid in the first place. One reason a marriage might not be valid is if the couple did not have _____ or always used _____, as this breaks the promise to accept children lovingly from God.

_____ is a legal agreement that a couple are no longer married and are now free to marry someone else. It is not accepted by the Catholic Church, as the married couple has promised before _____ to stay together 'till _____ do us part'. In addition, Jesus taught that anyone who divorced and then married another person was committing _____.

_____ is when a person who has been married before marries another person. The Catholic Church teaches that this should only happen when the original husband or wife has _____ or had an annulment. In the Catholic Church, a person who remarries without an annulment or their partner's death cannot receive _____.

B The text above gives some reasons why the Catholic Church is against divorce. Now answer the questions below.

1. Describe **one** situation where divorce might be the most compassionate solution.

   _____
   _____
   _____
   _____

2. Give another reason why some people think that divorce should be allowed.

   _____
   _____
   _____
   _____

Chapter 4: **Theme A: Religion, relationships and ethical studies**

Exam practice

Use your answers to the previous two activities to help you answer this exam question. The source of religious belief and teaching on page 65 might also be helpful.

Explain **two** contrasting views on divorce.

Refer to scripture or another source of Christian belief and teaching in your answer. **[5 marks]**

_____
_____
_____
_____
_____
_____
_____
_____
_____
_____

TIP
It makes sense for one of your views to be Christian, as you have to refer to a source of Christian belief and teaching in your answer. But your contrasting view could be Christian or it could be non-religious, or even come from a different religion.

Activity 4.7: Family planning and contraception

pages 276–277

During a Catholic wedding, the couple promises that they will accept children lovingly from God. Every act of sex within their marriage should be both unitive and procreative.

Answer the following questions about family planning and contraception in sentences.

1. Why does the Catholic Church teach that using artificial contraception is wrong?

_____
_____
_____
_____

Chapter 4: **Theme A: Religion, relationships and ethical studies**

2. What is natural family planning?
   _____
   _____
   _____
   _____

3. Why does the Catholic Church accept natural family planning?
   _____
   _____
   _____
   _____

> **TIP**
> Think carefully about why the Catholic Church is against artificial contraception but accepts natural family planning. What is the difference that makes one acceptable but the other wrong?

4. Name a Christian Church that accepts the use of contraception.
   _____

5. Give **two** reasons why some people agree with the use of artificial contraception.

   1 _____
   _____

   2 _____
   _____

Activity 4.8: The nature and purpose of the family

pages 278–279

Answer the following questions about family in sentences.

1. For Catholics, one purpose of the family is to procreate (produce children). Another purpose is to love and support each other. Give **two** more purposes of the family for Catholics.

   1 _____
   _____

   2 _____
   _____

69

Chapter 4: **Theme A: Religion, relationships and ethical studies**

2. There are different types of family. In the table below, write down whether the following descriptions are about:

   an extended family   a nuclear family   a family with same-sex parents

	This is the structure of most Catholic families in the UK.
	This type of family is not encouraged by the Catholic Church, as the Church teaches that marriage should be between a man and woman.
	Some Catholic children in the UK have this type of family structure, as they live with their parents and grandparents.

3. Give **three** morals or values that you think the Catholic Church would want children to be taught by their parents.

   1 _____

   2 _____

   3 _____

4. Explain why the Catholic Church believes that the family is the best environment in which to bring up children.

   _____
   _____
   _____

Exam practice

Now answer this exam question.

Explain **two** contrasting beliefs in contemporary British society about the issue of same-sex parenting.
- You must refer to a Christian belief or view.
- Your contrasting belief may come from Christianity or from another religious or non-religious tradition.   **[4 marks]**

TIP
This question means you need to give one view about same-sex parenting and develop it. You then need to give a contrasting (different) view about same-sex parenting and develop it. One of your views must be Christian.

70

Chapter 4: Theme A: Religion, relationships and ethical studies

Activity 4.9: Roles within the family

page 280

A Using the boxes on the right-hand side, fill in the gaps in the sentences below to help you complete the quotation from *Ephesians* 5:21 and 6:4, NRSV.

"Be s_____ to one another out of reverence for Christ.

W_____, be subject to your husbands as you are to the Lord.

For the husband is the head of the wife just as C_____ is the head of the church …

Husbands, love your wives, just as Christ l_____ the church and gave himself up for her …

Children, obey your p_____ in the Lord, for this is right.

'H_____ your father and mother' – this is the first commandment with a promise: 'so that it may be well with you and you may live long on the earth.'

And, fathers, do not provoke your c_____ to anger, but bring them up in the discipline and instruction of the L_____."

- People should live family lives as if they are serving Jesus.
- Wives should show their love by doing what their husbands ask.
- Husbands should love their wives unconditionally, so much they would be prepared to die for them.
- Children should honour their parents by obeying them as God commands it.
- Fathers should show love and kindness to children, so they should bring them up in the Christian faith.

B Now answer the following question.

1. A father goes out to work while a mother stays at home to look after their new baby. In this situation, how might each parent show that they are being 'subject to one another'?

Chapter 4: Theme A: Religion, relationships and ethical studies

Activity 4.10: Roles and responsibilities within the family

pages 280–281

Mark the following statements about the Catholic Church's views on roles and responsibilities in the family as true or false.

Statement	True	False
The Catholic Church believes the mother's role in looking after the home and children is very important.	☐	☐
The Catholic Church teaches that the husband's work is more important than the wife's work.	☐	☐
The Catholic Church teaches that men and women are equal but have different roles within the family.	☐	☐
Catholic parents should show love and kindness to their children.	☐	☐
Catholic children should honour their parents by disobeying them.	☐	☐
Traditionally, one of the husband's roles in a Catholic family is to take care of the home.	☐	☐
Traditionally, one of the husband's roles in a Catholic family is to provide an income for the family.	☐	☐

Activity 4.11: Gender equality in the Bible

pages 282–283

A Read this text about gender equality in the Bible, written as a response to the statement 'The Bible teaches that men and women are equal'. Five of the sentences are incorrect. As you read, highlight these five sentences (the first one has been done for you, so there are four left to find).

The Bible teaches that God created men and women equal. ==This is shown in the creation story in Genesis 1, where only men are described as being created in the image of God.== Throughout the Old Testament, there are examples of women playing special roles, such as Deborah who acted as judge. Another famous woman in the Old Testament was Ruth who showed Buddhists how to be faithful.

Also in the New Testament Jesus showed little respect for women. For example, in his teachings on divorce he said that the same standards apply to men and women, which was unusual at the time. Jesus also appeared first to a woman after the resurrection.

However, some people note that there is a much greater focus on men in the Bible, for example the twelve apostles were all male. Another argument that men are considered more important than women is based on the second creation story in Genesis 2. In this story, the woman was made second out of Adam's hair. Although in response to this, others point out that later in the same chapter it stresses that men and women combined are the 'full' form of a human being.

In summary, there are many more stories about women than men in the Bible. However, this reflects a society where women had little or no power or education. Against this background, the Bible gives a much greater acknowledgement of the role of women than could be expected, and Paul explicitly teaches that male and female are 'one in Christ Jesus'. This shows that men and women in the Bible are equal according to God.

Chapter 4: Theme A: Religion, relationships and ethical studies

B Now rewrite the five sentences below so they are correct. The first one has been done for you.

Sentence 1: *This is shown in the creation story in Genesis 1, where both men and women are described as being created in the image of God.*

Sentence 2: _____

Sentence 3: _____

Sentence 4: _____

Sentence 5: _____

Sources of religious belief and teaching

page 283

A Learn the following quotation.

> "there is no longer male and female; for you are all one in Christ Jesus"
> *Galatians* 3:28, NRSV

This quotation is from Paul's teaching in the Bible. It shows that men and women are equally valued by Christ.

Fill in the gaps below. It will help you to learn the quotation if you say the whole thing out loud every time you write it.

"there is no _____ male and _____ ; for you are all _____ in Christ _____ "

Now cover up the text above and have a go at writing out the whole quotation from memory.

" _____ "

B Now answer the following question.

1. What do you think Paul meant when he wrote 'there is no longer male and female'?

_____
_____
_____
_____

73

Chapter 4: Theme A: Religion, relationships and ethical studies

Key terms

pages 282–287

A These terms and their meanings are muddled up. Write out the meanings in the correct order in the second table below.

Gender equality	Producing children
Gender prejudice	The practice of controlling how many children a couple might have and when they have them
Gender discrimination	People are given equal rights whatever their sex
Artificial contraception	Not treating one sex as equal, for example not giving women the same opportunities as men
Family planning	Unnatural methods used to prevent a pregnancy from taking place
Procreation	Judging someone unfairly based on their sex

Gender equality	
Gender prejudice	
Gender discrimination	
Artificial contraception	
Family planning	
Procreation	

B Now write the correct term beside each meaning. For an extra challenge, cover up the rest of this activity and try to see if you can recall the words from memory.

People are given equal rights whatever their sex	
Judging someone unfairly based on their sex	

74

Chapter 4: **Theme A: Religion, relationships and ethical studies**

The practice of controlling how many children a couple might have and when they have them	
Not treating one sex as equal, for example not giving women the same opportunities as men	
Producing children	
Unnatural methods used to prevent a pregnancy from taking place	

Sources of religious belief and teaching

page 285

A Learn the following quotation from Pope Francis.

> "God endowed men and women with identical dignity as persons […] Equal dignity and equal rights, nevertheless, do not mean uniformity."
> *Youcat* 401

This quotation from Youcat shows that the Catholic Church believes men and women are equally important but that they have different roles to play.

Fill in the gaps below. It will help you to learn the quotation if you say the whole thing out loud every time you write it.

"God _____ men and _____ with identical _____ as persons […] Equal dignity and _____ rights, nevertheless, do not mean _____."

Now cover up the text above and have a go at writing out the whole quotation from memory.

"_____
_____
_____"

B Now answer the following question.

1. How does the quotation show that the Catholic Church believes men and women are complementary?

_____
_____
_____

75

Chapter 4: **Theme A: Religion, relationships and ethical studies**

Activity 4.12: Gender prejudice and discrimination

pages 286–287

A Mark these statements about gender prejudice and discrimination as true or false.

	True	False
Women are allowed to be priests in the Catholic Church.	☐	☐
The Catholic Church teaches that women should have equal pay for equal work.	☐	☐
The Catholic Church teaches that a woman's most important role is to bring up her children.	☐	☐
The Catholic Church teaches that equality means men and women should always be treated identically.	☐	☐
The Catholic Church teaches that some roles belong to one gender rather than the other.	☐	☐

B Which of the following statements do you think expresses the most important Catholic teaching on men and women? Underline your choice.

- Men and women were created equal by God.
- Men and women have their own roles and should not be treated identically.
- Women should be allowed to stay at home and bring up their children.
- Men and women have the same rights, such as equal pay for equal work.
- Only men are allowed to be priests.

TIP
There is no correct answer as such here, but you need to be able to give reasons for the answer you choose.

C Now give **two** reasons for your choice.

1 _____

_____

_____

2 _____

_____

_____

76

Chapter 4: Theme A: Religion, relationships and ethical studies

Exam practice

Use your answers to Activities 4.9–4.12 to write a complete answer to this exam question.

'The Catholic Church does not view men and women as equal.'

Evaluate this statement. In your answer you:

- should give reasoned arguments in support of this statement
- should give reasoned arguments to support a different point of view
- should refer to Christian arguments
- may refer to non-religious arguments
- should reach a justified conclusion.

[12 marks]

> **! REMEMBER…**
>
> Focus your answer on the statement you are asked to evaluate.
>
> - Try to write at least three paragraphs – one with arguments to support the statement, one with arguments to support a different point of view, and a final paragraph with a justified conclusion stating which side you think is more convincing, and why.
> - Look at the bullet points in the question, and make sure you include everything that they ask for.
> - The key skill that you need to demonstrate is evaluation. This means expressing judgements on the arguments that support or oppose the statement, based on evidence. You might decide an argument is strong because it is based on a source of religious belief and teaching, such as a teaching from the Bible, or because it is based on scientific evidence. You might decide an argument is weak because it is based on a personal opinion, or a popular idea with no scientific basis. You can use phrases in your chains of reasoning such as 'I think this a convincing argument because…' or 'In my opinion, this is a weak argument because…'.

Chapter 4: **Theme A: Religion, relationships and ethical studies**

Key Terms Glossary

As you progress through the course, you can collect the meanings of useful terms in the glossary below. You can then use the completed glossaries to revise from.

To do well in the exam you will need to understand these terms and include them in your answers. Tick the shaded circles to record how confident you feel. Use the extra boxes at the end to record any other terms that you have found difficult, along with their definitions.

- ○ I recognise this term
- ○ I understand what this term means
- ● I can use this term in a sentence

Divorce

Adultery

Equality

Annulment

Family planning

Artificial contraception

Gender discrimination

Atheist

Gender prejudice

Cohabitation

Homosexuality

79

Chapter 4: Theme A: Religion, relationships and ethical studies

Humanist

Sex before marriage

Marital

Theology of the Body

Marriage

Unitive

Procreative

Remarriage

Sanctity of marriage vows

Chapter 5: Theme B: Religion, peace and conflict

Activity 5.1: Biblical perspectives on violence

pages 290–291

Fill in the gaps in the sentences below using some of the words provided. (There are more words than gaps – you will have to decide which ones to leave out.)

anger   murder   Joseph   peace   God   Jesus   violence   Abel   good   war

The book of Genesis includes a story of the first ever _____, when Cain killed his brother _____. Because of this, _____ told Cain that he was cursed.

This tells us that, even though everything was created to be _____, _____ is a part of human nature and often leads to _____.

Jesus taught that these parts of human nature should be avoided to allow people to live in _____.

Exam practice

Now answer the exam question below.

Which **one** of the following committed the first murder according to the book of Genesis? **[1 mark]**

Put a tick (✓) in the box next to the correct answer.

A Adam ☐

B Cain ☐

C Abel ☐

D Eve ☐

Chapter 5: **Theme B: Religion, peace and conflict**

Sources of religious belief and teaching

pages 290–291

A Learn some quotations about anger and peace.

> "if you are angry with a brother or sister, you will be liable to judgement"
> *Matthew* 5:22, NRSV

In the Sermon on the Mount (a famous talk that Jesus gave to his followers), Jesus taught that anger is wrong and will result in God's judgement.

Fill in the gaps below. It will help you to learn the quotation if you say the whole thing out loud every time you write it.

"if you are _____ with a _____ or _____,

you will be _____ to _____"

Now cover up the text above and have a go at writing out the whole quotation from memory.

"_____

_____"

> "Peace I leave with you; my peace I give to you."
> *John* 14:27, NRSV

Jesus said these words to his disciples at the Last Supper. For Christians, the word 'peace' doesn't just mean not fighting, it means a deep feeling of wellbeing and inner calm that helps people to accept changes and challenges in life with a feeling of security and trust.

Fill in the gaps below to help you learn this second quotation.

"_____ I leave with you; my _____ I _____

to you."

Now cover up the text above and have a go at writing out the whole quotation from memory.

"_____"

B Now answer the question below.

1. What does the Bible teach about peace? In your answer, refer to at least one of the quotations above.

_____
_____
_____
_____
_____

Chapter 5: **Theme B: Religion, peace and conflict**

Activity 5.2: Forgiveness and reconciliation

pages 292–293

Answer the questions below in sentences.

A Forgiveness

Jesus taught that forgiveness should be limitless (people should forgive 'seventy-seven times', not 'seven times').

1. Write down **one** more teaching that Jesus gave about forgiveness.
   _____
   _____
   _____

Jesus forgave Peter when Peter turned his back on Jesus.

2. Give **one** more example of when Jesus showed forgiveness.
   _____
   _____
   _____

3. Do you think that Christians should forgive criminals today? Explain your answer, referring to Jesus' teachings.
   _____
   _____
   _____
   _____

B Reconciliation

1. What does 'reconciliation' mean?
   _____
   _____

Jesus taught that reconciliation leads to peace, which he prayed for at the Last Supper by saying 'Peace I leave with you; my peace I give to you'.

2. Write down **one** more teaching that Jesus gave about reconciliation.
   _____
   _____
   _____

3. A set of twins has fallen out after arguing about where to hold their joint birthday party. How could they be reconciled?
   _____
   _____
   _____

Chapter 5: Theme B: Religion, peace and conflict

Activity 5.3: Christian attitudes towards justice

pages 294–295

A Read this text about Christian attitudes towards justice.

Justice means:
- bringing about what is right or fair according to the law
- making up for a wrong that has been committed.

Justice is an essential part of God's Kingdom, so it is important for Christians to try to create justice to help spread God's Kingdom on earth. The importance of justice is shown in the Old Testament when the prophet Amos says:

'let justice roll down like waters and righteousness like an ever-flowing stream.' (*Amos* 5:24)

There are many examples in history of people being treated unjustly. One example is in South Africa during the second half of the twentieth century, when black people were discriminated against throughout society. Wherever people are denied justice, Christians have a responsibility to take action to give them justice. Pope Benedict XV said:

'Building a just and civil order […] is an essential task that every generation must take up […] the Church is duty bound to [understand] the requirements of justice.' (*Deus Caritas Est* 28)

B Now answer the following questions.

1. What does the word 'justice' mean?
   _____
   _____

2. Why do Christians think that it is important to create justice?
   _____
   _____
   _____
   _____

3. Give **one** example of people being treated unjustly.
   _____
   _____

4. Copy out one of the two quotations from above and then explain what you think it means.

   Quotation: _____
   _____
   _____

   Meaning: _____
   _____
   _____

TIP
Try to really understand the meaning of any quotations you learn. This will help you to use them in a relevant way in the exam.

Activity 5.4: Righteous anger and violent protest

page 295

Some Christians use the term 'righteous anger' to describe anger that they think is acceptable. They believe that showing anger towards a situation which God would not approve of is justified if the anger is:

- controlled
- used to encourage positive change.

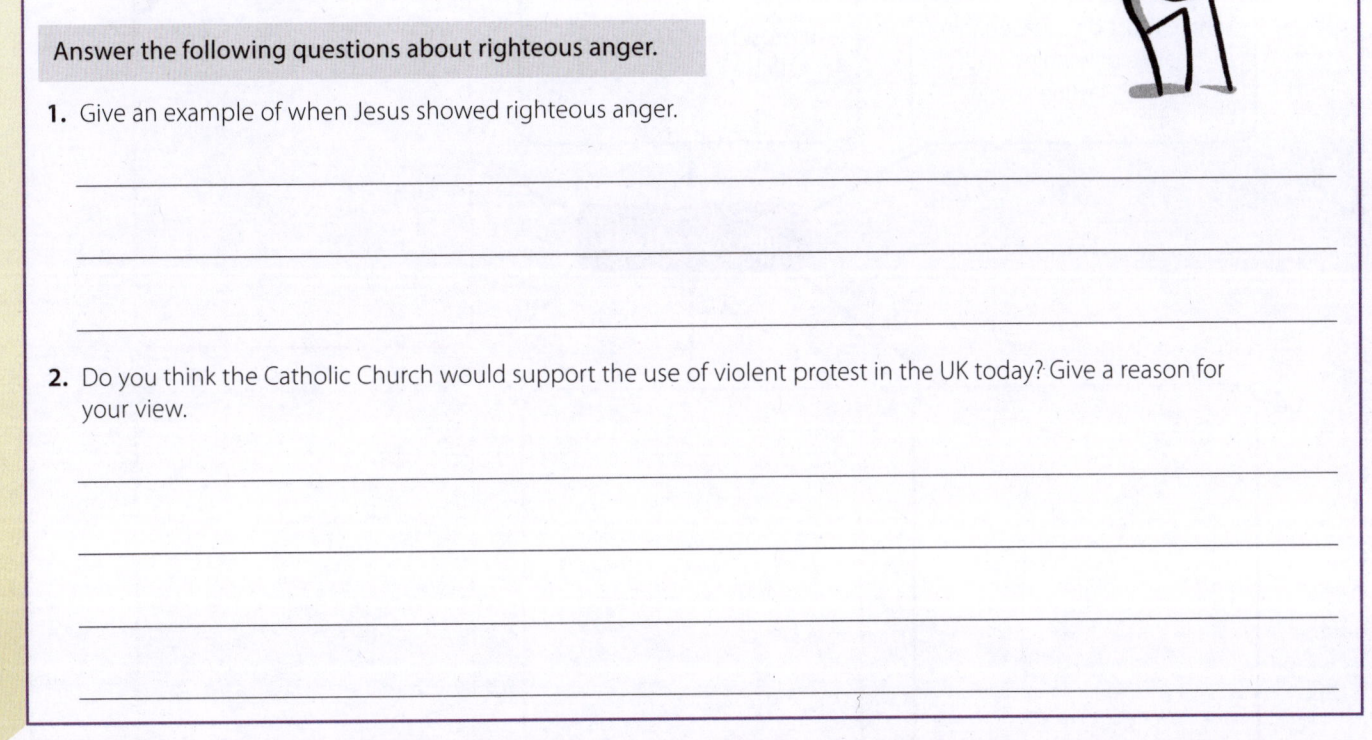

Answer the following questions about righteous anger.

1. Give an example of when Jesus showed righteous anger.

   _____
   _____
   _____

2. Do you think the Catholic Church would support the use of violent protest in the UK today? Give a reason for your view.

   _____
   _____
   _____
   _____

Exam practice

Now answer this exam question.

Explain **two** contrasting beliefs in contemporary British society about anger.

- You must refer to a Christian belief or view.
- Your contrasting belief may come from Christianity or from another religious or non-religious tradition. **[4 marks]**

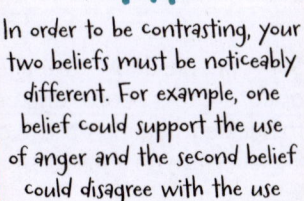

_____
_____
_____
_____
_____
_____
_____

TIP

In order to be contrasting, your two beliefs must be noticeably different. For example, one belief could support the use of anger and the second belief could disagree with the use of anger.

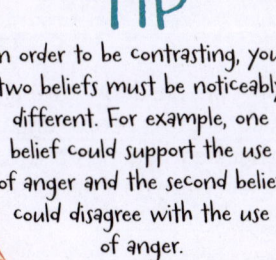

Chapter 5: **Theme B: Religion, peace and conflict**

Activity 5.5: Just war theory

pages 296–297

A According to the just war theory, there are six criteria that a war has to fulfil in order to be 'just'. Two of these are given below. Complete the spider diagram by adding in the remaining four criteria.

- There must be a reasonable chance of winning and bringing lasting peace.
- It must have a just cause (such as self-defence).

Just war criteria

B Now answer the following questions.

1. Which of these six criteria do you think is most important for a war to be considered 'just'? Give a reason for your choice.

_____
_____
_____
_____

2. Some people think that war can never be 'just', and it is always better to find other options. Other people disagree and think that the just war theory is a useful way to decide when it is right to go to war. What is your opinion on the just war theory? Explain why you agree or disagree with it in the space below.

_____
_____
_____
_____

TIP
There is no right or wrong answer to either of these questions, but it is important that you can explain your answer by giving reasons for what you think.

86

Chapter 5: **Theme B: Religion, peace and conflict**

Activity 5.6: Contrasting views in Britain about nuclear weapons and WMD

pages 298–299

A Read the argument below in favour of nuclear weapons and weapons of mass destruction (WMD). Then, in the blank speech bubble, write an argument for why Britain should not have nuclear weapons or WMD.

> It is good for Britain to have nuclear weapons and weapons of mass destruction. This deters others from attacking Britain. Such weapons are also important for self-defence, especially as other countries have them.

B Now answer the following questions.

1. Which of the views above do you think most Catholics would agree with? Give a reason why.

   _____
   _____
   _____

2. Which of the views above do you agree with? Give a reason why.

   _____
   _____
   _____

TIP
It is useful to remember the idea of 'nuclear deterrence'. This is when a country has nuclear weapons in order to deter (discourage) other countries from attacking it. It is one of the main reasons why Britain has nuclear weapons.

Sources of religious belief and teaching

page 299

Learn the following quotation.

> ❝Nothing is lost by peace; everything may be lost by war.❞
>
> *Pope Pius XII*

This quotation sums up the Catholic Church's attitude towards war and the use of nuclear weapons. It shows that the Church prefers a peaceful approach wherever possible.

Fill in the gaps below. It will help you to learn the quotation if you say the whole thing out loud every time you write it.

❝ _____ is lost by _____ ; everything may be _____ by _____ . ❞

Now cover up the text above and have a go at writing out the whole quotation from memory.

❝ _____
_____ ❞

87

Chapter 5: Theme B: Religion, peace and conflict

Activity 5.7: The consequences of modern warfare

pages 300–301

A Read the text below about the consequences of modern warfare, and the Catholic Church's views on these consequences.

Consequence	The Catholic Church's views
There will be civilian casualties	Civilians must be protected. 'Non-combatants, wounded soldiers and prisoners must be respected and treated humanely' (Catechism of the Catholic Church 2313).
Refugees will be forced to flee from danger	People who are fleeing fighting must be welcomed and protected by all countries. 'We cannot insist too much on the duty of giving foreigners a hospitable reception. It is a duty imposed by human solidarity and Christian charity.' (*Populorum Progressio* 67)
The environment will be harmed	Warfare damages the planet and is against the responsibilities of stewardship. 'Delicate ecological balances are upset by the uncontrolled destruction of animal and plant life.' (Pope John Paul II, Message for the World Day of Peace 1990)

B Now answer the following questions.

1. Explain what 'civilian casualties' means.

2. How does the Catholic Church think countries should respond to refugees fleeing from a war?

3. Explain why modern warfare goes against the responsibilities of stewardship.

4. Give **one** reason why some people think there are some situations when weapons of mass destruction should be used.

Chapter 5: Theme B: Religion, peace and conflict

Exam practice

Now answer the exam question below.

'Weapons of mass destruction should never be used.'

Evaluate this statement. In your answer you:

- should give reasoned arguments in support of this statement
- should give reasoned arguments to support a different point of view
- should refer to Christian arguments
- may refer to non-religious arguments
- should reach a justified conclusion.

[12 marks]

> **! REMEMBER...**
>
> Focus your answer on the statement you are asked to evaluate.
>
> - Try to write at least three paragraphs – one with arguments to support the statement, one with arguments to support a different point of view, and a final paragraph with a justified conclusion stating which side you think is more convincing, and why.
> - Look at the bullet points in the question, and make sure you include everything that they ask for.
> - The key skill that you need to demonstrate is evaluation. This means expressing judgements on the arguments that support or oppose the statement, based on evidence. You might decide an argument is strong because it is based on a source of religious belief and teaching, such as a teaching from the Bible, or because it is based on scientific evidence. You might decide an argument is weak because it is based on a personal opinion, or a popular idea with no scientific basis. You can use phrases in your chains of reasoning such as 'I think this a convincing argument because…' or 'In my opinion, this is a weak argument because…'.

Chapter 5: **Theme B: Religion, peace and conflict**

Activity 5.8: Violence and war in the Old Testament

pages 302–303

A Read the text below about violence and war in the Old Testament.

The Old Testament contains several instances of war, some of which helped the Israelites to settle in the Promised Land and to defend it from attack. The Israelites could be seen as a persecuted group who were fighting for the survival of their faith.

Exodus 21:24, NRSV teaches 'eye for eye, tooth for tooth', which seems to justify returning violence with violence. However, at the time this was written it was an attempt to reduce violence, so a punishment only applied to those who had done something wrong – not to their families or tribes as well.

Many Old Testament passages show that God's wish is for peace. For example, *Isaiah* 2:4, NRSV looks forward to a time when weapons are unnecessary, and 'nation shall not lift up sword against nation'.

B Using the points above, write a paragraph explaining what the Old Testament teaches Christians today about war and violence.

_____
_____
_____
_____
_____
_____
_____
_____

TIP
Do you think that a Christian reading the Old Testament today would get the impression that war and violence are good or bad? Think about whether there are certain situations where war and violence are more acceptable than others.

Activity 5.9: Holy war

page 303

In Christianity, a holy war is a war that has been approved by a major religious leader (usually the Pope), and is intended to defend the Christian faith from attack. It is not part of current Christian belief but it is an idea that has been used in the past.

Answer the following questions about holy war.

1. The Crusades are the best known example of a holy war. What was the purpose of the Crusades?

_____
_____
_____
_____
_____

Chapter 5: **Theme B: Religion, peace and conflict**

2. Do you think the Bible supports the idea of holy war? Give a reason for your answer.

   _____
   _____
   _____
   _____

   TIP
   Activity 5.8 will help you to answer this question, but think also about Jesus' teachings in the New Testament.

3. Do you think most Christians today agree with holy war? Give a reason for your answer.

   _____
   _____
   _____
   _____

Exam practice

Use your answers to the previous two activities to help you answer this exam question.

Explain **two** Christian beliefs about holy war.

Refer to scripture or another source of Christian belief and teaching in your answer. **[5 marks]**

_____
_____
_____
_____
_____
_____
_____
_____
_____
_____
_____

Chapter 5: Theme B: Religion, peace and conflict

Activity 5.10: Pacifism

pages 304–305

A Read this information about approaches to war and peace within Christianity.

Jesus	Quakers	Pope Francis
Jesus taught 'if anyone strikes you on the right cheek, turn the other also' (*Matthew* 5:39, NRSV). When Jesus was arrested he told his disciples to 'Put your sword back into its place; for all who take the sword will perish by the sword' (*Matthew* 26:52, NRSV).	In the First World War, a Christian group called Quakers refused to fight but became stretcher bearers and treated the wounded in battle instead.	Pope Francis supports peace and urges people to pray for peace, but does acknowledge that on occasions, limited force should be used in self-defence or to defend the weak.

B Now answer the following questions.

1. What is pacifism?

   _____
   _____

2. Do you think the following figures or groups could be described as pacifists? Give a reason for your answer.

   Jesus: _____
   _____
   _____

   Quakers: _____
   _____
   _____

   Pope Francis: _____
   _____
   _____

3. Do you think it is possible to agree with the just war theory and be a pacifist? Give a reason for your answer.

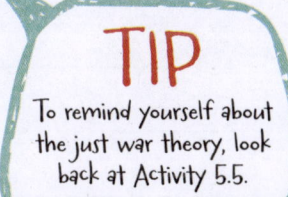

   _____
   _____
   _____
   _____

TIP
To remind yourself about the just war theory, look back at Activity 5.5.

93

Chapter 5: **Theme B: Religion, peace and conflict**

Activity 5.11: The Catholic Church's response to war

pages 306–307

A Read this text that describes some of the things Pope Francis has done to try to achieve peace.

Every week Pope Francis leads large crowds in prayer, often beginning with prayers for peace.

In 2014, he organised a prayer meeting between the leaders of Israel and Palestine. Using Jewish and Muslim prayers, he hoped that bringing them together in prayer would bring about change.

Also in 2014, he organised a football match in Rome to raise money for children who were victims of war. International players from a number of different faiths took part.

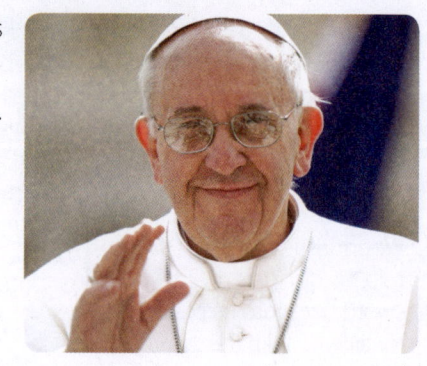

B Now answer the questions below in sentences.

1. Choose **one** of these actions and explain whether you think it is an effective way to bring about peace.

2. Pope Francis once said that 'Peacemaking calls for courage, much more than warfare.' He also said that 'War is irrational; its only plan is to bring destruction'.

    Choose **one** of these two quotations and say whether you agree with it or not, giving reasons why.

C CAFOD, Aid to the Church in Need and Caritas International are three Catholic agencies that help the victims of war. Choose **one** of these agencies and give an example of the work it has done to help the victims of war.

Chapter 5: Theme B: Religion, peace and conflict

Exam practice

Now answer the following exam question.

Name **two** Catholic agencies that respond to victims of war. **[2 marks]**

1 _____
  _____

2 _____
  _____

Activity 5.12: Terrorism

pages 308–309

Terrorism means to use unlawful violence, usually against innocent civilians, in order to achieve a political goal.

Below are four quotations that help to explain why the Catholic Church opposes terrorism. Explain how each quotation says that terrorism is wrong. One example has been done for you.

Source of religious belief and teaching	How does this quotation oppose terrorism?
"Let every person be subject to the governing authorities […] whoever resists authority resists what God has appointed, and those who resist will incur judgement." *Romans* 13:1-2, NRSV	This quotation says that someone who goes against the government goes against God, and will face his judgement as a result. Terrorists go against the government by unlawfully harming people, so they will be judged harshly for this.
"never avenge yourselves, but leave room for the wrath of God" *Romans* 12:19, NRSV	
"You shall not murder" *Exodus* 20:13, NRSV	
"Terrorism threatens, wounds, and kills indiscriminately; it is gravely against justice and charity" Catechism of the Catholic Church 2297	

Chapter 5: Theme B: Religion, peace and conflict

Activity 5.13: Torture, radicalisation and martyrdom

pages 310–311

A Read the text below about torture, radicalisation and martyrdom.

Explanation	Catholic teaching
Torture The use of severe physical or psychological pain to punish someone or to force them to do or say something. Considered wrong because it: • is illegal, even in war • denies the victim their human rights • is barbaric and inhuman. Could be justified if it prevents a terrorist attack.	"Torture which uses physical or moral violence to extract confessions, punish the guilty, frighten opponents, or satisfy hatred is contrary to respect for the person and for human dignity." *Catechism of the Catholic Church 2297*
Radicalisation Adopting extreme views on religious, social or political issues. Considered wrong because it: • can make people unwilling to accept alternative views • threatens unity in society and can lead to terrorist actions • may be a result of feeling rejected from society/religion. Society should work to tackle inequality and prevent people from feeling rejected.	"In the past, cultural differences have often been a source of misunderstanding between peoples and the cause of conflicts and wars." *Pope John Paul II, Message for the World Day of Peace, 1990*
Martyrdom Someone who suffers or dies because of their beliefs. Considered wrong because it: • can be seen as a needless waste of life • could encourage others to suffer or die. Christian martyrs are usually people who have been put to death for refusing to give up their Christian beliefs.	"If any want to become my followers, let them deny themselves and take up their cross and follow me." *Matthew 16:24, NRSV* "A Christian martyr is a person who is ready to suffer violence or even to be killed for Christ, who is the truth, or for a conscientious decision made on the basis of faith." *Youcat 454*

B Now answer the questions below in sentences.

1. Explain your views on these three issues. Do you agree or disagree with each one? Why or why not?

   Torture: _____

   _____

   _____

   Radicalisation: _____

   _____

   _____

   Martyrdom: _____

   _____

   _____

Chapter 5: **Theme B: Religion, peace and conflict**

2. Do you think the Catholic Church would agree with your views? Explain your answers.

Torture: _____

_____

_____

Radicalisation: _____

_____

_____

Martyrdom: _____

_____

_____

Key terms

pages 312–313

A These terms and their meanings are muddled up. Write out the meanings in the correct order in the second table below.

Peacemaking	Opposing a government without using violence
Conflict resolution	Showing grace and mercy, and pardoning someone for what they have done wrong
Non-violent resistance	The action of trying to establish peace
Forgiveness	Resolving a dispute between two people or groups by creating peace between them

Peacemaking	
Conflict resolution	
Non-violent resistance	
Forgiveness	

97

Chapter 5: **Theme B: Religion, peace and conflict**

B Now write the correct term beside each meaning. For an extra challenge, cover up the rest of this activity and try to see if you can recall the words from memory.

Showing grace and mercy, and pardoning someone for what they have done wrong	
Opposing a government without using violence	
Resolving a dispute between two people or groups by creating peace between them	
The action of trying to establish peace	

Activity 5.14: Catholic organisations working for peace   pages 312–313

Fill in the gaps in the sentences below using some of the words provided. (There are more words than gaps – you will have to decide which ones to leave out.)

diocese   illness   France   negotiations   Britain   conventional
justice   nuclear   fifty   respect   violence   one hundred

Pax Christi was founded after the Second World War to create understanding between _____

and Germany. It now works in more than _____ countries to establish peace that is based on

respect, _____ and reconciliation. It tries to settle disputes peacefully before there is any need for

_____ .

The **Justice and Peace Commission** was founded in _____

in 1978, and works with each _____ of the Catholic Church.

It focuses on treating people with _____ and campaigns

for the removal of _____ weapons from the world. It tries

to remove war by removing the causes of war.

98

Chapter 5: **Theme B: Religion, peace and conflict**

Key Terms Glossary

As you progress through the course, you can collect the meanings of useful terms in the glossary below. You can then use the completed glossaries to revise from.

To do well in the exam you will need to understand these terms and include them in your answers. Tick the shaded circles to record how confident you feel. Use the extra boxes at the end to record any other terms that you have found difficult, along with their definitions.

- ○ I recognise this term
- ○ I understand what this term means
- ● I can use this term in a sentence

Bullying _____

Conflict resolution _____

Dignity _____

Forgiveness _____

Holy war _____

Justice _____

Just war theory _____

Martyrdom _____

Non-violent resistance _____

Nuclear deterrence _____

Nuclear war _____

99

Chapter 5: Theme B: Religion, peace and conflict

Pacifism _____

Peacemaking _____

Radicalisation _____

Reconciliation _____

Righteous anger _____

Terrorism _____

Torture _____

Violence _____

Violent protest _____

Weapons of mass destruction _____

Chapter 6: Theme C: Religion, human rights and social justice

Activity 6.1: Human dignity in the Bible
pages 316–317

Dignity means being worthy of honour and respect. For each of the quotations from the Bible below, explain how you think it shows that Christians believe all people should have dignity.

TIP
The first two quotations in this table are particularly useful to remember. You can use them in your exam to help explain why humans should have dignity.

Teaching	What does this teach about human dignity?
"God created humankind in his image, in the image of God he created them; male and female he created them" *Genesis* 1:27, NRSV	
"You shall love your neighbour as yourself" *Mark* 12:31, NRSV	
"There is no longer Greek and Jew, circumcised and uncircumcised […] slave and free; but Christ is all and in all!" *Colossians* 3:11, NRSV	
"What does the Lord require of you but to do justice, and to love kindness, and to walk humbly with your God?" *Micah* 6:8, NRSV	

Activity 6.2: Freedom of religion or belief
page 317

Answer the following questions about freedom of religion or belief.

1. In most countries in the world, a basic human right is the right to 'freedom of religion or belief'. What do you think this means?

   _____
   _____
   _____

TIP
A 'basic human right' is something that everyone in the world should have access to, like clean water or an education.

2. In the UK, do you think everyone has the right to freedom of religion or belief? Explain your answer.

   _____
   _____
   _____
   _____

101

Chapter 6: Theme C: Religion, human rights and social justice

3. Do you agree that people should have the right to follow any religion they choose? Explain your answer.

_____
_____
_____
_____
_____
_____

4. The Catholic Church has said that 'no one is to be forced to act in a manner contrary to his own beliefs'. Do you think this means the Catholic Church agrees with the right to freedom of religion or belief? Explain your answer.

_____
_____
_____
_____
_____
_____
_____
_____

Activity 6.3: Human rights in *Gaudium et Spes* 26

pages 318–319

A The Catholic Church sets out its teachings on human rights in *Gaudium et Spes* 26. Draw lines to connect the three quotations from *Gaudium et Spes* 26 with their correct meanings.

Quotation	Meaning
"the common good […] involves rights and duties with respect to the whole human race"	Every person should have dignity because humans are superior to all other living beings.
"there is a growing awareness of the exalted dignity proper to the human person, since he stands above all things"	Society must be built on truth and justice, and motivated by love.
"This social order […] must be founded on truth, built on justice and animated by love"	People's rights and duties are the same all over the world and should be respected and protected.

102

B Now answer the following questions.

1. Two of the rights that *Gaudium et Spes* 26 says all people should have are the right to food and the right to respect. Give **two** more rights listed in *Gaudium et Spes* 26.

   1 _____

   2 _____

2. *Gaudium et Spes* 26 says that it is important for people to have human rights in order to have dignity. Do you agree with this? Explain why.

   _____
   _____
   _____
   _____

3. *Gaudium et Spes* 26 says it is important to work to improve society, as this is necessary to make sure everyone has access to basic human rights. In the UK, one way that Christians might help to improve access to basic human rights is by volunteering at a food bank, which helps to supply some of the poorest families with food. Give another way that Christians in the UK can help to improve access to basic human rights.

   _____
   _____
   _____

Activity 6.4: Rights and responsibilities

pages 320–321

A In the left-hand column, write whether the definition is a right or a responsibility. Then give an example of each in the right-hand column.

Right/Responsibility	Definition	Example
	Something a person is expected to do.	
	A freedom that all people are entitled to.	

B Add the words 'right' and 'responsibility' to the sentence below so it makes sense.

Governments are expected to give everyone a _____ to education. This gives young people the _____ to allow others to learn, for example by not disrupting lessons.

103

Chapter 6: Theme C: Religion, human rights and social justice

C Now answer the following questions.

1. For everyone to have basic human rights, people need to take responsibility to respect those rights and to help create access to them. For example, for someone to have the right to privacy, their employer has to take responsibility to be careful with their private information.

   Give another example of how rights and responsibilities are linked.

   _____
   _____
   _____
   _____

2. Name a Catholic agency that works to give people human rights, and give one example of how it does this.

   _____
   _____
   _____
   _____

Activity 6.5: Responsibilities of wealth

pages 322–323

A Tick the following statements about wealth to show whether you think the Catholic Church would agree with them or not.

	Agree	Disagree
Having money or wealth is bad.	☐	☐
Christians should use their wealth to help others.	☐	☐
Christians should not get too attached to money.	☐	☐
All Christians should be poor.	☐	☐
There should be more equality in the world, rather than extremes between rich and poor.	☐	☐
Christians should use their wealth to have a good time.	☐	☐
Helping the poor helps to give them more dignity.	☐	☐

Chapter 6: **Theme C: Religion, human rights and social justice**

B Now answer these questions.

1. Explain how Christians think money should be used.

_____
_____
_____

2. *1 Timothy* 6:10, NRSV says: 'For the love of money is a root of all kinds of evil'. Why do you think the 'love of money' is considered to be wrong?

_____
_____
_____
_____

> **TIP**
> *1 Timothy* 6:10, NRSV says 'For the love of money is a root of all kinds of evil.' This warns against greed. If you just write 'money is the root of all kinds of evil' in your exam, you will not earn any credit because the quotation is incomplete and no longer about greed.

3. Christians believe that stewardship of wealth is important. Explain what 'stewardship of wealth' means.

_____
_____
_____
_____
_____

105

Chapter 6: Theme C: Religion, human rights and social justice

Activity 6.6: Wealth creation and exploitation

pages 324–325

A Fill in the gaps in the sentences below using the words provided. (There are more words than gaps – you will have to decide which ones to leave out.)

| wealth | duty | greed | expense | advantage | exploitation | slavery |
| poor | rich | Christians | opportunity | Church | work |

Creating _____ is important for people's survival. It helps people provide for their families and where possible, the wider community.

Catholics believe they have a _____ to create wealth to help other people. The Church teaches that Catholics should do what they can to ensure people live in a stable and supported environment.

This means that wealth should not be pursued because of _____ for money. Gaining wealth at the _____ of others is against the teachings of the Catholic Church.

The creation of wealth should also not harm other people. Rich nations and international companies often take _____ of the needs of poorer people, who cannot easily stand up for themselves.

The Catholic Church teaches that _____ of the poor is wrong. Human trafficking (modern-day _____) is an example of exploitation. Factories in the clothing industry where workers are paid very little to work long hours are a form of exploitation of the _____.

B In two sentences, summarise what the Catholic Church teaches about wealth creation.

_____
_____
_____
_____

Chapter 6: Theme C: Religion, human rights and social justice

Activity 6.7: The wealth of the Catholic Church

page 325

Answer the following questions about the wealth of the Catholic Church.

1. Give **two** ways that the Catholic Church helps the poor.

   1 _____
   _____

   2 _____
   _____

2. Give **two** things that the Catholic Church needs to spend some of its wealth on aside from helping the poor.

   1 _____
   _____

   2 _____
   _____

3. Do you think these things are more important than helping the poor? Or should that money be spent on helping the poor instead? Explain your answer.

   _____
   _____
   _____
   _____

4. The Catholic Church is very wealthy. A lot of its wealth is in its land, buildings and art. Give **one** reason why it might be difficult for the Catholic Church to spend more of its wealth on helping the poor.

   _____
   _____
   _____

5. The Catholic Church teaches that wealth should be used to help others. Do you think it is wrong for the Church to have so much wealth? Explain your answer.

   _____
   _____
   _____
   _____

Chapter 6: Theme C: Religion, human rights and social justice

Exam practice

Now answer the exam question below.

'The Catholic Church should spend more of its wealth on helping the poor'.

Evaluate this statement. In your answer you:

- should give reasoned arguments in support of this statement
- should give reasoned arguments to support a different point of view
- should refer to Christian arguments
- may refer to non-religious arguments
- should reach a justified conclusion. **[12 marks]**

! REMEMBER…

Focus your answer on the statement you are asked to evaluate.

- Try to write at least three paragraphs – one with arguments to support the statement, one with arguments to support a different point of view, and a final paragraph with a justified conclusion stating which side you think is more convincing, and why.
- Look at the bullet points in the question, and make sure you include everything that they ask for.
- The key skill that you need to demonstrate is evaluation. This means expressing judgements on the arguments that support or oppose the statement, based on evidence. You might decide an argument is strong because it is based on a source of religious belief and teaching, such as a teaching from the Bible, or because it is based on scientific evidence. You might decide an argument is weak because it is based on a personal opinion, or a popular idea with no scientific basis. You can use phrases in your chains of reasoning such as 'I think this a convincing argument because…' or 'In my opinion, this is a weak argument because…'.

Chapter 6: **Theme C: Religion, human rights and social justice**

Activity 6.8: Ideas about greed

pages 326–327

Fill in the blank boxes below to show different ideas and beliefs about greed.

Greed is a desire to have more of something.		
	Jesus taught greed was wrong when he said 'Be on your guard against all kinds of greed' (Luke 12:15, NRSV).	

Exam practice

Now answer this exam question.

Explain **two** Christian beliefs about greed.

Refer to scripture or another source of Christian belief and teaching in your answer. **[5 marks]**

_____
_____
_____
_____
_____
_____
_____
_____
_____
_____
_____

110

Activity 6.9: Materialism and the vow of poverty

pages 326–327

The Catholic Church teaches that:

- all people have dignity and value.
- people should focus on helping others.
- it is important to take care of the world and protect the environment.

A Use these teachings to explain why the Catholic Church is against materialism.

_____
_____
_____
_____
_____
_____

B Monks, nuns and some other Christians take a vow of poverty to commit themselves to fully serving God. Read the text below that gives some of the arguments for and against taking a vow of poverty.

Agree with taking a vow of poverty	Disagree with taking a vow of poverty
Shows full commitment to God, and follows Jesus' advice to 'sell your possessions, and give the money to the poor' (*Matthew* 19:21, NRSV).	Money and wealth can be used to help others; the Bible teaches that the 'love of' money is wrong rather than money itself (*1 Timothy* 6:10).
Helps to solve the imbalance of wealth in the world.	People who have families to provide for can't easily take a vow of poverty.
Leads to greater happiness without the stress and worry caused by money and possessions.	It is right to enjoy possessions that are bought with money earned through hard work.

C Now answer the following question.

1. How important do you think it is for Christians to take a vow of poverty? Explain your answer.

_____
_____
_____
_____
_____
_____
_____

111

Chapter 6: Theme C: Religion, human rights and social justice

Activity 6.10: The preferential option for the poor

pages 328–329

Answer the following questions about the preferential option for the poor.

1. The Church teaches that Christians should put the needs of poor people before others, and focus most on helping them. Give **two** reasons why you think the Church wants to put the needs of poor people before others.

   1 _____
   _____

   2 _____
   _____

> **TIP**
> The Church teaching that poor people should be put first is called 'the preferential option for the poor'. This teaching appears in a Church document written by Pope Francis called *Evangelii Gaudium*. Try to remember the meaning of these two phrases.

2. In *Evangelii Gaudium* 198, Pope Francis wrote 'I want a Church which is poor and for the poor'. Give **two** ways that a local church could show it is 'for the poor'.

   1 _____
   _____

   2 _____
   _____

3. Pope Francis also wrote that the poor have 'much to teach us' because they 'know the suffering Christ'. What do you think this means?

   _____
   _____
   _____
   _____

Sources of religious belief and teaching

page 328

Learn the following quotation.

> **"** Let each of you look not to your own interests, but to the interests of others. Let the same mind be in you that was in Christ Jesus. **"**
> *Philippians* 2:4, NRSV

This quotation shows that Christians should follow Jesus' example and help others. It is one of the teachings behind the preferential option for the poor.

Fill in the gaps below. It will help you to learn the quotation if you say the whole thing out loud every time you write it.

" Let each of you _____ not to your own _____, but to the interests of _____. Let the same _____ be in you that was in _____ Jesus. **"**

112

Now cover up the text on the previous page and have a go at writing out the whole quotation from memory.

" _____

_____

_____ "

Exam practice

Now answer the following exam question.

Give **two** teachings about the preferential option for the poor. **[2 marks]**

1 _____

_____

2 _____

_____

Activity 6.11: Ways that Christians can help the poor

pages 330–331

The Catholic Church believes that Christians have a duty to fight poverty and to help the poor. Fill in the spider diagram below to show some of the different ways that Christians can help the poor.

Giving money to a charity that helps the poor, like the St Vincent de Paul Society.

Ways to help the poor

113

Chapter 6: **Theme C: Religion, human rights and social justice**

Activity 6.12: The responsibility to help those in poverty
page 331

A Read the statements below and tick the boxes to show whether you agree or disagree with them.

	Agree	Disagree
Most people living in poverty do not need any help.	☐	☐
Only giving money to the poor does little to help because they come to rely on this aid.	☐	☐
Only governments and powerful organisations can help the poor.	☐	☐
People living in poverty should try harder to improve their situation.	☐	☐
Poverty is the fault of society, so it is society's responsibility to help the poor.	☐	☐
Buying more Fairtrade products is a good way to support the poor.	☐	☐

B For any of the statements you have disagreed with, use the space below to briefly explain why you disagree with them.

_____
_____
_____
_____
_____
_____
_____
_____

Activity 6.13: The work of CAFOD
pages 332–333

A Read the following text about CAFOD.

CAFOD is a Christian charity that works to relieve poverty in countries around the world. The work that CAFOD does includes:

- campaigning against exploitation and injustice
- providing poor people in developing countries with access to clean water
- providing short-term aid such as food and shelter after natural disasters
- supporting Fairtrade so workers get a fair price for their goods
- campaigning for the government to spend more money on aid.

B Now answer these questions.

1. Which **one** of these actions do you think might be most important to the Catholic Church?

_____
_____

TIP There is no correct answer here as such – what is more important is that you can explain your choice and provide evidence to back it up.

Chapter 6: **Theme C: Religion, human rights and social justice**

2. Why do you think this is the most important action?

_____
_____
_____

3. Is there any evidence you can use to support your choice? For example, a Catholic teaching or a quotation from the Bible? Write your evidence below.

_____
_____
_____

> **TIP**
> Christian Aid is another Christian charity that it is useful to know about. Like CAFOD, it helps people around the world to escape from poverty.

Exam practice

Now answer the exam question below.

Which **one** of the following is a Christian charity? **[1 mark]**

Put a tick (✓) in the box next to the correct answer.

A Action Aid ☐

B CAFOD ☐

C Oxfam ☐

D Save the Children ☐

Activity 6.14: Divergent views on helping the poor

pages 332–333

Fill in the gaps in the sentences below using the words provided. (There are more words than gaps – you will have to decide which ones to leave out.)

| causes | policies | poor | Christian | aid | rich |
| charities | churches | governments | developing | Oxfam | |

Some people in Britain donate their time or money to charities that work to tackle poverty, such as _____

or Save the Children. They believe this is an important way to help the _____.

Some people do not donate to _____. They believe that providing _____

is not the best way to solve the _____ of poverty. They prefer to campaign for

_____ to change their _____ in order to help people in the

_____ world.

115

Chapter 6: Theme C: Religion, human rights and social justice

Activity 6.15: Racial prejudice and discrimination

pages 334–335

Fill in the gaps in the sentences below using the words provided. (There are more words than gaps – you will have to decide which ones to leave out.)

hatred   respect   prejudice   negative   inferior   image   race
discrimination   saved   dignity   baptised   gender   positive

Racial _____ means having a negative attitude towards someone based on their _____. This becomes _____ when it turns into actions and behaviour.

The Catholic Church teaches that because all people are created in the _____ of God and are loved by God, they should be treated with _____. In addition, all people are _____ by the death and resurrection of Jesus, which gives them equal _____. This means that no one should be treated as _____ to anyone else.

Some people think that _____ discrimination is acceptable as it gives opportunities to people who have been discriminated against in the past.

Sources of religious belief and teaching

page 336

A Learn the following quotation.

> "In that renewal there is no longer Greek and Jew, circumcised and uncircumcised, barbarian, Scythian, slave and free; but Christ is all and in all!"
> *Colossians* 3:11, NRSV

This quotation shows that everyone is equally valued by Christ.

Fill in the gaps below. It will help you to learn the quotation if you say the whole thing out loud every time you write it.

"In that renewal there is no longer _____ and Jew, circumcised and _____, barbarian, Scythian, slave and _____; but _____ is all and in _____!"

TIP
You learned a similar quotation from Galatians 3:28 on page 73 in chapter 4. It is a useful quotation to remember when writing answers about equality.

Chapter 6: **Theme C: Religion, human rights and social justice**

Now cover up the text on the previous page and have a go at writing out the whole quotation from memory.

" _____

_____

_____ "

B Now answer the following question.

1. Do you think the quotation on the previous page is a good one to use to support the argument that racial prejudice and discrimination are wrong? Explain your answer.

_____
_____
_____

Activity 6.16: Equality

pages 336–337

A Read these statements and decide whether you think they are Catholic beliefs or not. Put a tick next to the statements you think are Catholic beliefs, and a cross next to those you think are not.

✓ or ✗

God created men to be superior to women. ☐

Men and women may have different roles but they are still of equal value and importance. ☐

Believing that men and women are equal makes all people the same. ☐

Homosexuals should not have sex because it cannot lead to conception. ☐

The Catholic Church should only have male priests, following Jesus' example. ☐

The Church of England agrees with the Catholic Church and also only has male priests. ☐

Having equal opportunities is an important part of all people being of equal value. ☐

Catholics believe that homosexuals should have rights and dignity as human beings. ☐

B In the space below, correct any statements that you have put a cross beside, so they do match Catholic beliefs.

_____
_____
_____
_____
_____
_____

117

Chapter 6: **Theme C: Religion, human rights and social justice**

Exam practice

Now answer this exam question.

Explain **two** contrasting beliefs in contemporary British society about equality.
- You must refer to a Christian belief or view.
- Your contrasting belief may come from Christianity or from another religious or non-religious tradition. **[4 marks]**

Key terms

pages 316–339

A These terms and their meanings are muddled up. Write out the meanings in the correct order in the second table on the next page.

Human rights	Being worthy of honour and respect
Justice	Unfairly judging someone before all the facts are known
Dignity	Actions or behaviours that are based on prejudice
Equality	The basic rights and freedoms to which all humans should be entitled
Prejudice	Ensuring society treats everyone fairly
Discrimination	Having equal rights and opportunities

118

Human rights	
Justice	
Dignity	
Equality	
Prejudice	
Discrimination	

B Now write the correct term beside each meaning. For an extra challenge, cover up the rest of this activity and try to see if you can recall the words from memory.

Actions or behaviours that are based on prejudice	
Having equal rights and opportunities	
Unfairly judging someone before all the facts are known	
Being worthy of honour and respect	
Ensuring society treats everyone fairly	
The basic rights and freedoms to which all humans should be entitled	

Chapter 6: **Theme C: Religion, human rights and social justice**

Activity 6.17: Justice, racial equality and racial prejudice

pages 338–339

A Read the following text about how Christians support justice and racial equality.

For Christians, the teaching 'love your neighbour' means treating people fairly and equally. This is an important way to promote equality and justice in a society.

In order for justice to be created, the laws of any country must respect every person living in that country, regardless of their race, colour, gender, etc. Christians have a responsibility to oppose any laws that consider some people to be less valuable than others.

The Catholic Church promotes tolerance and racial equality in a number of ways. Catholic schools welcome students of any faith or ethnicity to share in the atmosphere of acceptance and tolerance that exists within the school. When a Pope is elected, all Catholics accept him regardless of his nationality or age.

The Catholic Church also supports victims of racial prejudice. Churches often organise activities where people of different races can spend time together and learn to value each other. They might also support victims through prayers, group discussions and the sacrament of reconciliation.

> **TIP**
> 'Racial equality' means treating people of different races in the same way. 'Victims of racial prejudice' are people who have been treated badly because of their race.

B Now answer the following questions.

1. Explain how following the teaching 'love your neighbour' can help to create justice.

_____
_____
_____

2. Why should the laws of any country respect every person?

_____
_____
_____

3. Give **two** examples of how the Catholic Church promotes racial equality.

1 _____
_____

2 _____
_____

4. Give **two** examples of how the Catholic Church supports victims of racial prejudice.

1 _____
_____

2 _____
_____

Chapter 6: **Theme C: Religion, human rights and social justice**

Key Terms Glossary

As you progress through the course, you can collect the meanings of useful terms in the glossary below. You can then use the completed glossaries to revise from.

To do well in the exam you will need to understand these terms and include them in your answers. Tick the shaded circles to record how confident you feel. Use the extra boxes at the end to record any other terms that you have found difficult, along with their definitions.

- ○ I recognise this term
- ○ I understand what this term means
- ● I can use this term in a sentence

Greed _____

CAFOD _____

Human rights _____

Christian Aid _____

Human trafficking _____

Dignity _____

Justice _____

Exploitation _____

Materialism _____

Freedom of religion or belief _____

Positive discrimination _____

121

Chapter 6: Theme C: Religion, human rights and social justice

Poverty

Wealth creation

Preferential option for the poor

Racial discrimination

Racial equality

Racial prejudice

Stewardship of wealth

Chapter 7: Exam practice: Themes

Chapter 7: **Exam practice: Themes**

Test the 1-mark question

Example

1. Which **one** of the following terms describes a sexual relationship where at least one of the couple is married to somebody else? **[1 mark]**

   Put a tick (✓) in the box next to the correct answer.

   A Divorce ☐

   B Annulment ☐

   C Adultery ✓

   D Contraception ☐ ✓(1)

WHAT WILL THE QUESTION LOOK LIKE?

The 1-mark question will always be a **multiple-choice question** with four answers to choose from. Only one answer is correct. The question will usually start with the words **'Which one of the following...'**

HOW IS IT MARKED?

You will receive 1 mark for choosing the correct answer.

! REMEMBER...

Read the question carefully before making your choice. Even if you are not sure of the right answer, make a guess – you may get it right anyway.

Be aware that if you tick more than one box, you will receive no marks, even if one of your selected answers is correct.

Activity

2. Which **one** of the following gives the best explanation of the term 'pacifism'? **[1 mark]**

   Put a tick (✓) in the box next to the correct answer.

   A Refusing to take part in a war ☐

   B Fighting only in a just war ☐

   C Helping victims of war ☐

   D Fighting only in a holy war ☐

3. Which **one** of the following is the meaning of 'stewardship of wealth'? **[1 mark]**

   Put a tick (✓) in the box next to the correct answer.

   A Gaining large amounts of wealth ☐

   B Sharing wealth with the poor ☐

   C Spending wealth irresponsibly ☐

   D Saving money to become wealthy ☐

Chapter 7: Exam practice: Themes

Test the 2-mark question

> **WHAT WILL THE QUESTION LOOK LIKE?**
> The 2-mark question will always start with the words **'Give two...'** or **'Name two...'**, and a maximum of **2 marks** will be awarded.

Example

1. Give **two** conditions that must apply for a war to be called a 'just war'. **[2 marks]**
   1. *There must be a good chance of success.* ✓ (1)
   2. *War must be a last resort.* ✓ (1)

> **HOW IS IT MARKED?**
> The examiner is looking for two different, correct answers. For each correct response you will receive 1 mark.

> ⚠ **REMEMBER...**
> You need to give **two pieces of information** in your answer. Use the numbered lines to make sure you write two separate points. Don't just repeat yourself – make each point says something new.
>
> Keep your answers short. You only need to provide two facts or short ideas; **you don't need to explain them or express any opinions**.

Activity

2. Give **two** Christian ideas about the purpose of the family. **[2 marks]**

The sample answer below would get 1 mark because only one correct answer is given. Add a new Christian idea about the purpose of the family to make the answer worth 2 marks.

1. *It provides moral guidance.*
2. _____

> **TIP**
> For 2-mark questions like this one, you need to write more than one word for each answer, but you don't need to spend time writing complete sentences.

3. Give **two** ways that either CAFOD or Christian Aid help the poor. **[2 marks]**

1. _____
2. _____

4. Give **two** reasons why the Catholic Church is against torture. **[2 marks]**

1. _____
2. _____

Chapter 7: **Exam practice: Themes**

Test the 4-mark question

Example

1. Explain **two** contrasting beliefs in contemporary British society about racial discrimination.
   - You must refer to a Christian belief or view.
   - Your contrasting belief may come from Christianity or from another religious or non-religious tradition. **[4 marks]**

Christians believe that racial discrimination is wrong because it is unjust. ✓ (1) *Treating one race of people better than those of a different race is completely unfair because all people should be treated equally.* ✓ (1)

Some people believe that positive discrimination is just, ✓ (1) *because its intention is to treat people of poorly treated races better by giving them special help, such as by giving them jobs for which they are qualified but which they might not get otherwise.* ✓ (1)

WHAT WILL THE QUESTION LOOK LIKE?

The 4-mark question will always start with the words **'Explain two…'**, and a maximum of 4 marks will be awarded.

Questions are likely to ask for **two contrasting points** (which means they should be noticeably different). They will normally make reference to contemporary British society. One point of view must be Christian, while the other can be Christian or come from any other religion, or may be non-religious.

HOW IS IT MARKED?

This answer would gain 4 marks because it makes two different points, one of which is Christian. Both points clearly show extra detail.

! REMEMBER...

Provide two **contrasting** (different) beliefs. Try to show the examiner where each belief begins. For example, you could start your answer with 'Some Christians believe…' and then move on to your second point on a new line by saying something like 'Other Christians believe…' or 'Some Jews believe…'.

Try to **add detail** to each belief by giving an example or adding more explanation. Adding detail to your points in this way will earn you more marks.

Activity

2. Explain **two** contrasting beliefs in contemporary British society about same-sex marriage.
   - You must refer to a Christian belief or view.
   - Your contrasting belief may come from Christianity or from another religious or non-religious tradition. **[4 marks]**

The sample answer below would get 4 marks because there are two points that are clearly different (contrasting), each with extra detail. Add a tick next to each point. Then underline the extra detail that has been added to each point.

Many Christians, especially Protestant Christians, agree with same-sex marriage, although not all support same-sex weddings taking place in a church. They believe that if two people are in love, they have a right to be married regardless of their gender.

Other Christians, including many Catholics, believe that same-sex marriage is wrong. This is because it does not allow procreation, a main purpose of marriage, to take place naturally.

TIP

When you are asked to give contrasting beliefs, a good approach is to give one belief and then explain why some people think the opposite of this. For example, here the student has explained why some Christians agree with same-sex marriage for their first point. For a contrast they have explained why other Christians disagree with same-sex marriage.

Chapter 7: Exam practice: Themes

3 Explain **two** contrasting beliefs in contemporary British society about pacifism.
- You must refer to a Christian belief or view.
- Your contrasting belief may come from Christianity or from another religious or non-religious tradition.

[4 marks]

The sample answer below would get 2 marks because it makes one point and then adds extra detail to this point. It includes a reference to Christianity. Add a second point for a third mark. If you can add detail to that point with an appropriate example or more explanation, the complete answer will get 4 marks.

The Catholic Church believes that it is best to use non-violent approaches to end conflicts. ✓ **(1)** *Pope Francis stated this was the case when he said 'War never again! Never again war!'* ✓ **(1)**

> **TIP**
> Remember that your second point can come from a non-religious tradition. However, don't assume that an atheist belief or view must automatically disagree with a Christian belief or view. Make sure it is **contrasting** before you use it in your answer.

4 Explain **two** contrasting beliefs in contemporary British society about artificial contraception.
- You must refer to a Christian belief or view.
- Your contrasting belief may come from Christianity or from another religious or non-religious tradition.

[4 marks]

The sample answer below would get 2 marks for giving two different beliefs. Add detail to each point to gain 2 more marks.

One belief is the Catholic one that says that contraception is not allowed. ✓ **(1)**

> **TIP**
> It is a good idea to start your second point on a new line, to make it clear where it begins.

A contrasting belief of non-religious people is that using contraception is a responsible act as it stops unwanted pregnancy. ✓ **(1)**

Chapter 7: **Exam practice: Themes**

5 Explain **two** contrasting beliefs in contemporary British society about nuclear deterrence.
- You must refer to a Christian belief or view.
- Your contrasting belief may come from Christianity or from another religious or non-religious tradition. **[4 marks]**

6 Explain **two** contrasting beliefs in contemporary British society about greed.
- You must refer to a Christian belief or view.
- Your contrasting belief may come from Christianity or from another religious or non-religious tradition. **[4 marks]**

Chapter 7: **Exam practice: Themes**

Test the 5-mark question

Example

1. Explain **two** Catholic beliefs about sex before marriage.

    Refer to scripture or another source of Christian belief and teaching in your answer. **[5 marks]**

    One Catholic belief about sex before marriage is that it is wrong because virginity before marriage is valued. ✓ **(1)** *This makes the husband and wife feel special, privileged and loved in marriage.* ✓ **(1)** *In the youth catechism it says that love is so great, so sacred and so unique that young people should wait until they are married to have sex.* ✓ **(1)**

    A second Catholic belief is that sex before marriage devalues marriage ✓ **(1)** *because sex is no longer something special that is exclusively reserved for marriage.* ✓ **(1)**

WHAT WILL THE QUESTION LOOK LIKE?

The 5-mark question will always start with the words **'Explain two…'** and end with the words **'Refer to scripture or another source of Christian belief and teaching in your answer'**. A maximum of **5 marks** will be awarded.

HOW IS IT MARKED?

This answer would gain 5 marks because it makes two different points, and both points have extra detail. It also refers to a relevant source of Christian belief and teaching (the youth catechism).

⚠ REMEMBER…

The 5-mark question is similar to the 4-mark question, so try to make **two different points** and **add extra detail** to each of them.

The additional instruction in the question asks you to **'refer to scripture or another source of Christian belief and teaching in your answer'**. Try to think of a reference to the Bible or another religious text like the Catechism, the words of a prayer, or a quotation from a Catholic leader (such as the Pope) to back up one of your points. You only need one reference but can add more than one if you want.

Activity

2. Explain **two** Christian beliefs about conflict resolution.

    Refer to scripture or another source of Christian belief and teaching in your answer. **[5 marks]**

    The sample answer below would get 5 marks because there are two points with extra detail, and a reference to a source of belief and teaching. Add a tick next to each point. Then underline where each point has extra detail. Finally, draw a circle around a reference to Christian belief and teaching.

    Christians should work to help solve conflicts, because they believe that an end to war will be a sign of God's kingdom being present on earth.

    Christians also believe that problems are not solved by violence but by peaceful methods. They support this belief by quoting the words of Jesus, who said 'Love your enemies, do good to those who hate you (Luke 6:27, NRSV).'

Chapter 7: **Exam practice: Themes**

3 Explain **two** Christian beliefs about the freedom of religion or belief.

Refer to scripture or another source of Christian belief and teaching in your answer. **[5 marks]**

> The sample answer below would get 3 marks as there is one point with extra detail, and one simple point. There is no reference to scripture or another source of Christian belief and teaching. Try to gain the maximum of 5 marks by adding detail to the second point, and adding a source of Christian belief and teaching to either of the points – it doesn't matter which.

Firstly, Catholics believe that accepting the right to freedom of religion or belief is a way of accepting that people are created to be different. ✓(1) *An example of this is that some people believe different things from others and they should be allowed to.* ✓(1)

Secondly, Catholics think that nobody should be forced to accept any particular religion. ✓(1)

> **TIP**
> You don't need to quote a source of belief and teaching word-for-word, but try to say where it came from, for example, whether it came from the Bible, a document produced by the Church, a speech by the Pope, etc.

4 Explain **two** Christian beliefs about the role of women in Church leadership.

Refer to scripture or another source of Christian belief and teaching in your answer. **[5 marks]**

> The sample answer below would get 2 marks as there is one point with extra detail. Complete the answer by adding a second point with extra detail, as well as a reference to a source of Christian belief and teaching.

The Catholic Church does not allow women to be priests. ✓(1) *It believes that as Jesus was male, it is correctly following his example.* ✓(1)
The Church of England... _____

> **TIP**
> Your reference to a source of belief and teaching can be added to either point.

129

Chapter 7: Exam practice: Themes

5 Explain **two** of Jesus' teachings about forgiveness.

Refer to scripture or another source of Christian belief and teaching in your answer. **[5 marks]**

_____
_____
_____
_____
_____
_____
_____
_____
_____
_____
_____
_____

6 Explain **two** Christian beliefs about pacifism.

Refer to scripture or another source of Christian belief and teaching in your answer. **[5 marks]**

_____
_____
_____
_____
_____
_____
_____
_____
_____
_____
_____
_____

Chapter 7: Exam practice: Themes

Test the 12-mark question

Example

1. 'There is no good reason for a Christian to fight a war.'

    Evaluate this statement.

    In your answer you:
    - should give reasoned arguments in support of this statement
    - should give reasoned arguments to support a different point of view
    - should refer to Christian arguments
    - may refer to non-religious arguments
    - should reach a justified conclusion. **[12 marks]**

WHAT WILL THE QUESTION LOOK LIKE?

The 12-mark question will always ask you to **evaluate** a statement. The bullet points underneath the statement will tell you the things the examiner expects to see in your answer. Here, you need to give reasoned arguments for and against the statement. Some of your arguments should refer to Christianity. The final bullet will always ask you to 'reach a justified conclusion'.

HOW IS IT MARKED?

The examiner will mark your answer using the level descriptors (see below).

REMEMBER...

Evaluating means to make a judgement, using **evidence** to decide how convincing you find the statement to be.

You should consider **arguments in support of the statement**, and decide how convincing you think those are, giving at least one reason. You then need to consider **why some people might support a different point of view**, and decide how convincing they are, again giving at least one reason.

You might want to decide how convincing an argument is by considering where it comes from. Is it based on a source of Christian belief and teaching, such as a teaching from the Bible, or something advised by a religious leader? If so, you may decide this evidence strengthens the argument and therefore whether you would support or oppose the statement in the question.

You might decide an argument is weak because it is only a personal opinion, or a popular idea with no strong evidence to support it. This would make it difficult for you to use to support or oppose the statement in the question when reaching a judgement and you must **explain the reasons why you reach your judgements**.

To reach a **justified conclusion** you should consider both sides of the argument, and make your own judgement about which you find more convincing. You might conclude that each side has its own strengths. To make sure your conclusion is 'justified', you need to give **reasons or evidence to support your view**, but don't *just* repeat all the reasons and evidence you have already used.

TIP

In the Themes exam paper, there are no extra marks for SPaG (spelling, punctuation and grammar). However, you should still aim to write well, as this will help the examiner understand what you are trying to say.

Level descriptors

Level	
Level 1 (1–3 marks)	• Point of view with reason(s) stated in support.
Level 2 (4–6 marks)	• Reasoned consideration of a point of view. • A logical chain of reasoning drawing on knowledge and understanding of relevant evidence and information. OR • Recognition of different points of view, each supported by relevant reasons/evidence. • **Maximum of Level 2 if there is no reference to religion.**
Level 3 (7–9 marks)	• Reasoned consideration of different points of view. • Logical chains of reasoning that draw on knowledge and understanding of relevant evidence and information. • **Clear reference to religion.**
Level 4 (10–12 marks)	• A well-argued response, reasoned consideration of different points of view. • Logical chains of reasoning leading to judgement(s) supported by knowledge and understanding of relevant evidence and information. • **Reference to religion applied to the issue.**

Chapter 7: **Exam practice: Themes**

Logical chains of reasoning

The level descriptors state that to achieve the higher levels you need to show 'logical chains of reasoning' in your answer. This is not as difficult as it sounds. It simply refers to an argument where one idea connects logically to the next.

If you take an idea, develop it by giving more detail and explanation, then provide evidence that supports your idea, you will be demonstrating a logical chain of reasoning. Each step in your argument is a link: together they make a chain of reasoning.

This might already be part of your normal way of writing, even if the phrase is new to you.

You will find some examples in the sample answers that follow.

2 'Catholic children should learn about their faith from their parents at home.'

Evaluate this statement.

In your answer you:
- should give reasoned arguments in support of this statement
- should give reasoned arguments to support a different point of view
- should refer to Christian arguments
- may refer to non-religious arguments
- should reach a justified conclusion.

[12 marks]

Here are four sample answers to the question above. Each one would be awarded a different level. Read all four answers carefully and compare them with the level descriptors on page 131.

Level 1 sample answer

This is a Level 1 answer because:
- it expresses an opinion
- it gives a reason.

To improve this answer the student could:
- create a simple chain of reasoning by giving relevant examples
- include a different point of view with reasons.

I agree that Catholic children should learn about their faith from their parents at home. This is one of the purposes of the family and parents are best placed to do it.

TIP
Here the student agrees with the statement and supports this with the belief that educating their children is part of a parent's duties.

Chapter 7: **Exam practice: Themes**

Level 2 sample answer

This is a Level 2 answer because:
- it adds a little more reasoning and evidence
- it mentions a different point of view.

To improve this answer the student could:
- add more reasons
- use a logical chain of reasoning for each point of view.

I agree that Catholic children should learn about their faith from their parents at home. This is one of the purposes of the family and parents are best placed to do it. They have learned their faith throughout their life and children trust them.

However, they may not know enough about their faith to teach it to their children and they may get it wrong.

TIP
Starting an answer with 'I agree' can be helpful but you can start in diffferent ways if you wish e.g. 'Some Catholics agree...'

TIP
You might find it helps to structure your answer so all of the arguments to support the statement are grouped together, and all of the arguments to support a different view are grouped together – as the student has done here.

133

Chapter 7: Exam practice: Themes

Level 3 sample answer

This is a Level 3 answer because:
- there is a reasoned consideration of different points of view
- it contains chains of reasoning
- it includes a conclusion.

To improve this answer the student could:
- provide more detail in the chains of reasoning
- develop the conclusion further.

I agree that Catholic children should learn about their faith from their parents at home. This is one of the purposes of the family and parents are best placed to do it. They have learned their faith throughout their life, and children should follow the commandment to respect their parents by trusting them. Another good reason for parents to educate their children is because they are role models. A child, especially a young one, will spend a lot of time with their parents and will learn from what they do. For example, do they really love their neighbour or just say that you should?

However, parents may not know enough about their faith to teach it to their children or may get it wrong. Just because somebody is a Catholic doesn't mean they get everything right or understand everything about their faith. This is important because nobody wants to learn the wrong thing as this could give them problems in later life. On the other hand, priests know most about the Catholic faith but aren't allowed to have children because they are celibate, so they can't teach their own children about the faith because they don't have any. So ordinary Catholic parents have to do it instead.

Although there are others ways to learn the faith, I think parents are best at it.

TIP
This paragraph includes different reasons in support of the statement. Each one has some reasoning.

TIP
To write a Level 3 answer, you need to show 'clear reference to religion'. This can be achieved by using accurate religious terms (such as 'commandment') and including clear beliefs about God or other aspects of a religion (such as the fact that the special commitment that priests have to God means they are not allowed to have children).

TIP
The student has written a conclusion and expressed a judgement. To move to the next level the student should include reasons to justify their decision.

Level 4 sample answer

This is a Level 4 answer because:
- it is well argued
- it contains extra points, reasons and evidence that build on the chains of reasoning in the Level 3 answer
- it has a more reasoned conclusion.

I agree that Catholic children should learn about their faith from their parents at home. This is one of the purposes of the family and parents are best placed to do it. They have learned their faith throughout their life, and children should follow the commandment to respect their parents by trusting them. Teaching their children about the Catholic faith is a very important part of being a good parent.

Another good reason for parents to educate their children is because they are role models. A child, especially a young one, will spend a lot of time with their parents and will learn from what they do. For example, do they really love their neighbour or just say that you should? Being a good role model is also about how a parent treats their children. According to 'Familiaris Consortio', parents should pay special attention to children by helping them to develop their dignity and a respect and concern for their rights. This is why it is important that children should learn from their parents, provided their parents do the right thing.

However, parents may not know enough about their faith to teach it to their children or may get it wrong. Just because somebody is a Catholic doesn't mean they get everything right or understand everything about their faith. This is important because nobody wants to learn the wrong thing as this could give them problems in later life. On the other hand, priests know most about the Catholic faith but aren't allowed to have children because they are committed to celibacy, so they can't teach their own children about the faith because they don't have any. So ordinary Catholic parents have to teach their children about the faith instead.

The fact that many Catholics attend a Catholic school shows that parents may not be the best at teaching children about the faith. Catholic schools have specially trained teachers to do this and they are not likely to get it wrong. Even the atmosphere within a Catholic school is respectful of the faith, and they provide the opportunity to worship God regularly, which is a requirement of being a Catholic. Parents can do their best but some might say that Catholic schools do it better.

Although there are other ways to learn the faith, I think parents are best at it. People learn to be better human beings if they are treated with dignity and respect from an early age, and parents have the chance to do that as a child grows and develops.

TIP Referring to Christian sources of belief and teaching can help to support your arguments, and is a good way to show 'clear reference to religion'.

TIP Start a new paragraph for each new chain of reasoning that you write.

TIP Paragraphs 2, 3 and 4 all contain logical chains of reasoning. Each sentence is linked to the others in the paragraph.

TIP The student has written a 'justified conclusion' by giving their opinion on the statement, as well as a reason for their opinion.

Chapter 7: Exam practice: Themes

Activity

3 'The poor should be responsible for sorting out their own problems.'

Evaluate this statement.

In your answer you:

- should give reasoned arguments in support of this statement
- should give reasoned arguments to support a different point of view
- should refer to Christian arguments
- may refer to non-religious arguments
- should reach a justified conclusion.

[12 marks]

A Read the sample answer below.

I disagree that the poor should be responsible for sorting out their own problems. As we live in a society, everybody has a responsibility for helping those who are struggling to keep up. Many people are vulnerable and there can be many reasons why they are poor. They may be unable to work because they are sick or elderly so have no way of sorting out their problems. They may be homeless and have no way of getting a home because they cannot afford to. There is no way that they can cope.

Christians are taught to love their neighbour which means they should help anybody who needs help. Jesus said that if you help other people then it's like helping Jesus himself, and this will help you to have a good afterlife. This is good motivation to help everyone who needs help and not leave them to do it by themselves. Faith is useless unless it is backed up by actions. This includes helping the poor along with loving God. You cannot say you love God if you don't help those in need. This is a very strong argument because the reward of eternal life, which is gained through loving God, is the aim of all Christians.

Many poor people do not like having to rely on hand-outs from other people or charities. They would prefer to provide for themselves but for some reason do not have the opportunity to do so. Giving them this opportunity is the best way that Christians can help them. This could mean giving them a job if they are able to work, so they can have a feeling of satisfaction that they are using their talents to provide for themselves. Jesus told the parable of the talents in which he praised those who used their talents to gain more rather than just relying on others. So some Christians would say that the poor need to take some responsibility for getting out of poverty, like working hard at a job if the opportunity is given to them.

Although Christians are taught to help the poor, it is the method of helping that is important. Providing opportunities to enable the poor to help themselves is more helpful than just giving them money, but in many cases, giving money helps them to reach a position where they can begin to help themselves. This is a challenge for all Christians.

TIP
This answer begins with an argument that supports a different point of view, instead of supporting the statement. This is a perfectly acceptable way of answering.

Chapter 7: **Exam practice: Themes**

B Now answer the following questions about the sample answer opposite.

1. Write down **two** of the arguments used to oppose the statement.

2. Do you agree that these are strong arguments? Why or why not?

3. Summarise the argument made in support of the statement.

4. The question says you should 'refer to Christian arguments'. Using a coloured pen, highlight any references to Christian teaching that you can find.

    Underline any phrases where the student is evaluating how convincing the arguments are.

5. The question asks you to reach a 'justified conclusion'. Do you think the last paragraph is a good 'justified conclusion'? Explain your answer.

137

Chapter 7: Exam practice: Themes

4 'Religious believers should have an important role in twenty-first-century conflicts.'

Evaluate this statement.

In your answer you:

- should give reasoned arguments in support of this statement
- should give reasoned arguments to support a different point of view
- should refer to Christian arguments
- may refer to non-religious arguments
- should reach a justified conclusion.

[12 marks]

The answer below is a Level 1 answer because it gives a point of view and has a couple of simple reasons to support it. In the space below, turn this into a Level 2 answer. You could do this by either:

- explaining further what religious believers could do and why they might do it. Try to do this in such a way as to turn what the student has written into a 'logical chain of reasoning'

or:

- adding a different point of view, with a reason to support it.

I agree that religious believers should have an important role in twenty-first-century conflicts. They could perhaps be a voice for peace and also help those who are injured.

Chapter 7: **Exam practice: Themes**

Now rewrite your answer so it is likely to achieve at least Level 3. To do this, you should:

- provide more reasons and evidence to support the statement. For example, you could refer to Christian teachings about working for peace and justice, fighting in wars (the just war theory), or helping victims of war
- make a reasoned argument for why religious believers should not have an important role, perhaps because they are less likely to fight (and why this may be)
- include a clear reference to religion. For example, you could include teachings from the Bible to support your arguments for or against the statement
- attempt to write a conclusion, possibly by making the reasoned point that fighting and trying to resolve conflicts peacefully may both be important.

TIP
Try to include logical chains of reasoning in your answer (see page 132).

139

Chapter 7: Exam practice: Themes

5 'The Catholic Church is right not to allow same-sex marriages.'

Evaluate this statement.

In your answer you:

- should give reasoned arguments in support of this statement
- should give reasoned arguments to support a different point of view
- should refer to Christian arguments
- may refer to non-religious arguments
- should reach a justified conclusion.

[12 marks]

> **! REMEMBER...**
>
> Focus your answer on the statement you are asked to evaluate.
>
> - Try to write at least three paragraphs – one with arguments to support the statement, one with arguments to support a different point of view, and a final paragraph with a justified conclusion stating which side you think is more convincing, and why.
> - Look at the bullet points in the question, and make sure you include everything that they ask for.
> - The key skill that you need to demonstrate is evaluation. This means expressing judgements on the arguments that support or oppose the statement, based on evidence. You might decide an argument is strong because it is based on a source of religious belief and teaching, such as a teaching from the Bible, or because it is based on scientific evidence. You might decide an argument is weak because it is based on a personal opinion, or a popular idea with no scientific basis. You can use phrases in your chains of reasoning such as 'I think this is a convincing argument because…' or 'In my opinion, this is a weak argument because…'.

Chapter 7: Exam practice: Themes

6 'Christians should do more to create equality between people.'

Evaluate this statement.

In your answer you:

- should give reasoned arguments in support of this statement
- should give reasoned arguments to support a different point of view
- should refer to Christian arguments
- may refer to non-religious arguments
- should reach a justified conclusion. **[12 marks]**

OXFORD
UNIVERSITY PRESS

Great Clarendon Street, Oxford, OX2 6DP, United Kingdom

Oxford University Press is a department of the University of Oxford.

It furthers the University's objective of excellence in research, scholarship, and education by publishing worldwide. Oxford is a registered trade mark of Oxford University Press in the UK and in certain other countries

© Oxford University Press 2019

The moral rights of the authors have been asserted

First published in 2019

All rights reserved. No part of this publication may be reproduced, stored in a retrieval system, or transmitted, in any form or by any means, without the prior permission in writing of Oxford University Press, or as expressly permitted by law, by licence or under terms agreed with the appropriate reprographics rights organization. Enquiries concerning reproduction outside the scope of the above should be sent to the Rights Department, Oxford University Press, at the address above.

You must not circulate this work in any other form and you must impose this same condition on any acquirer

British Library Cataloguing in Publication Data

Data available

978-0-19-844497-8

10 9 8 7 6 5 4 3 2 1

Paper used in the production of this book is a natural, recyclable product made from wood grown in sustainable forests.

The manufacturing process conforms to the environmental regulations of the country of origin.

Printed in India by Manipal Technologies Limited

Acknowledgements
We are grateful to the authors and publishers for use of extracts from their titles and in particular for the following:

The Scripture quotations contained herein are from **The Revised Standard Version of the Bible: Catholic Edition**, copyright © 1965, 1966 the Division of Christian Education of the National Council of the Churches of Christ in the United States of America. Used by permission. All rights reserved.

Excerpts from **Tanakh: The Holy Scriptures** (Jewish Publication Society Inc., 1991). © 1985, The Jewish Publication Society, Philadelphia. Reproduced with permission from University of Nebraska Press.

Excerpts from **Catechism of the Catholic Church**, http://www.vatican.va/archive/ccc_css/archive/catechism/ccc_toc.htm (Strathfield, NSW: St Pauls, 2000). © Libreria Editrice Vaticana. Reproduced with permission from The Vatican; **Pope Benedict XVI: Deus Caritas Est**, December 25th 2005 (The Vatican, 2005). © Libreria Editrice Vaticana. Reproduced with permission from The Vatican; **Pope Francis:** Twitter post, September 2nd 2013, https://twitter.com/pontifex/status/374466943312330753 (The Vatican, 2013). © Libreria Editrice Vaticana. Reproduced with permission from The Vatican; **Pope Francis: Evangelii Gaudium**, On the Proclamation of the Gospel in Today's World, November 24th 2013, (The Vatican, 2013). © Libreria Editrice Vaticana. Reproduced with permission from The Vatican; **Pope Francis: Invocation for Peace**, Speech at the Vatican Gardens, June 8th 2014, (The Vatican, 2014). © Libreria Editrice Vaticana. Reproduced with permission from The Vatican; **Pope Francis: Homily**, Mass at the Military Memorial of Redipuglia, September 13th 2014, (The Vatican, 2014). © Libreria Editrice Vaticana. Reproduced with permission from The Vatican; **Pope John XXIII: Pacem in Terris**, On Establishing Universal Peace in Truth, April 11th 1963 (The Vatican, 1993). © Libreria Editrice Vaticana. Reproduced with permission from The Vatican; **Pope John Paul II: Message for the World Day of Peace**, January 1st 2001 (The Vatican, 2001). © Libreria Editrice Vaticana. Reproduced with permission from The Vatican; **Pope Paul VI: Dignitatis Humanae**, On the Right of the Person and of Communities to Social and Civil Freedom in Matters Religious, December 7th, 1965 (The Vatican, 1965). Reproduced with permission from The Vatican. © Libreria Editrice Vaticana; **Pope Paul VI: Gaudium et Spes**, Pastoral Constitution on the Church in the Modern World, December 7th, 1965 (The Vatican, 1965). © Libreria Editrice Vaticana. Reproduced with permission from The Vatican.; **Pope Paul VI: Encyclical Populorum Progressio: Encyclical of Pope Paul Vi on the Development of Peoples**, (The Vatican, 1967). © Libreria Editrice Vaticana. Reproduced with permission from The Vatican; **Dignitatis Humanae, 2**; **YOUCAT: YOUCAT**, (Ignatius Press, 2011). Reproduced with permission from Ignatius Press.

Cover: Hands of God and Adam, detail from The Creation of Adam, from the Sistine Ceiling. 1511 (fresco) (pre restoration), Buonarroti, Michelangelo (1475–1564)/Vatican Museums and Galleries, Vatican City/Bridgeman Images.

Artworks: Jason Ramasami & QBS Learning.

Photos: p23: Martin Metsemakers/Shutterstock; **p37:** paula sierra/Getty Images; **p63:** giulio napolitano/Shutterstock; **p68:** BraunS/iStock; **p94:** Philip Chidell/Shutterstock; **p98:** Mark Kerrison/Alamy Stock Photo; **p105:** Cesar Okada/iStock; **p106:** Purepix/Alamy Stock Photo; **p120:** Martin Allinger/Shutterstock.

We have made every effort to trace and contact all copyright holders before publication, but if notified of any errors or omissions, the publisher will be happy to rectify these at the earliest opportunity.

Links to third party websites are provided by Oxford in good faith and for information only. Oxford disclaims any responsibility for the materials contained in any third party website referenced in this work.

Please note that the practice questions in this book allow students a genuine attempt at practising exam skills, but they are not intended to replicate examination papers.

Thank you
OUP wishes to thank Matthew Dell, Rabbi Benjy Rickman and Julie Haigh for their help reviewing this book.